Demand-Driven Inventory Management

Table of Contents

Chapter 1: Introduction to Demand-Driven Inventory Management

In the fast-evolving landscape of modern business, traditional inventory management models are often strained under the complexities of volatile consumer demand, global supply chains, and shifting market dynamics. This chapter provides an in-depth look at demand-driven inventory management, a forward-thinking approach that is transforming inventory practices across industries. By aligning inventory decisions with real-time customer demand, demand-driven inventory management addresses the limitations of conventional systems and enables businesses to be more agile, responsive, and efficient.

Overview of Demand-Driven Inventory Management

Demand-driven inventory management (DDIM) is a system where inventory levels are guided primarily by real-time demand signals rather than forecasts or historical data alone. Unlike traditional models, which rely heavily on static inventory settings and projected demand estimates, DDIM is a responsive model that leverages demand insights to optimize inventory levels dynamically. This approach enables companies to better match inventory supply with actual customer needs, significantly reducing the risk of overstocking, stockouts, and obsolete inventory.

In a demand-driven model, inventory decisions are tightly integrated with customer orders and other real-time demand indicators. This alignment helps companies maintain the right level of stock at the right place and time, which is essential for managing costs, improving service levels, and responding swiftly to market fluctuations. DDIM involves several key components:

Real-Time Data and Analytics: Demand-driven inventory relies on real-time data from sales, point-of-sale (POS) systems, and supply chain sensors to provide accurate demand signals. Advanced analytics are applied to interpret this data, offering insights into demand patterns and enabling informed decision-making.

Responsive Replenishment: Unlike the static, forecast-based replenishment of traditional models, DDIM emphasizes frequent, responsive replenishment cycles. This ensures that inventory levels stay in tune with current demand, minimizing the need for excessive safety stock.

Strategic Buffering: In a demand-driven approach, strategic buffering is used to protect inventory from demand variability and lead time uncertainties. Instead of stockpiling inventory across all product lines, buffers are set based on demand volatility, product criticality, and lead times, resulting in a more efficient use of resources.

Demand Sensing and Demand Shaping: Demand sensing is the process of using short-term demand signals to adjust inventory in real time, while demand shaping involves influencing customer demand through promotions, pricing adjustments, and marketing strategies. Together, these practices allow companies to respond to fluctuations in demand while optimizing inventory.

By implementing a demand-driven approach, companies achieve greater inventory flexibility, enhance customer satisfaction, and improve their overall operational efficiency. DDIM's responsive nature also facilitates faster adaptation to external disruptions, making it a resilient choice in today's unpredictable market environment.

Differences from Traditional Inventory Models

To fully appreciate the benefits of demand-driven inventory management, it's essential to understand how it differs from traditional inventory models. Traditional models, such as the Economic Order

Quantity (EOQ) and fixed-order-point systems, are generally based on historical data and static reorder points. While these systems have worked well in the past, they are increasingly inadequate for handling the demands of today's dynamic markets.

Here are some of the key differences:

Forecast-Driven vs. Demand-Driven:

Traditional models rely heavily on forecasts to determine inventory levels. Forecasting is inherently uncertain and can lead to issues like overstocking and stockouts if the predictions are inaccurate. These models often use historical data and seasonality to predict future demand, assuming that past patterns will continue in the future.

Demand-driven models, in contrast, rely on actual demand signals and real-time data rather than forecasts alone. This shift allows for a more accurate alignment of inventory with current demand, reducing reliance on assumptions and static demand projections.

Static vs. Dynamic Inventory Levels:

In traditional models, inventory levels are set based on fixed reorder points and economic order quantities, which can lead to inefficiencies in volatile markets. These levels may not adjust quickly enough to respond to sudden changes in demand, creating the risk of either excess inventory or shortages.

Demand-driven models use dynamic inventory levels that can be adjusted based on real-time data, making them more adaptable. Inventory quantities are continually optimized based on demand patterns, helping businesses to better manage resources and reduce carrying costs.

Replenishment Frequency:

Traditional inventory models typically follow fixed replenishment cycles or batch ordering, often dictated by supplier schedules or preset intervals. This approach can result in inefficiencies, especially in fast-moving industries, as it lacks flexibility and fails to account for fluctuating demand.

Demand-driven inventory management promotes more frequent, agile replenishment cycles. By receiving smaller quantities more often, companies can align their inventory more closely with customer demand, reducing lead times and minimizing the need for high safety stocks.

Buffer Management:

In traditional models, buffer stock or safety stock is usually calculated based on historical data and predetermined thresholds, which do not account for rapid changes in the marketplace.

Demand-driven models employ strategic buffering, where inventory buffers are set based on demand volatility and product criticality. This selective buffering approach is more efficient, as it focuses resources on high-priority items and critical stock-keeping units (SKUs).

Supply Chain Visibility:

Traditional inventory systems often operate in silos, lacking visibility across the entire supply chain. This limited view can lead to delays, as companies are unable to quickly adapt to changes upstream or downstream.

Demand-driven inventory management emphasizes end-to-end visibility, allowing organizations to track demand, inventory levels, and shipments in real-time. This enhanced visibility improves communication and collaboration across the supply chain, leading to more efficient operations.

These differences highlight the core advantage of a demand-driven approach: its flexibility and responsiveness to changes in customer demand. By leveraging real-time data and focusing on customer-driven replenishment, demand-driven models offer a distinct advantage in today's complex and fast-paced market environment.

Importance of a Demand-Driven Approach in Today's Market

In recent years, demand-driven inventory management has gained prominence as companies face an increasingly volatile and interconnected global market. Here are some of the key reasons why a demand-driven approach is essential for success:

Adaptability to Market Volatility:

The business environment is more unpredictable than ever, influenced by rapid technological advancements, economic shifts, and geopolitical factors. Demand patterns can shift quickly, and companies that rely solely on forecasts struggle to adapt to these changes.

Demand-driven inventory management enables companies to respond quickly to changes, providing the flexibility to adjust inventory based on real-time insights. This adaptability reduces the risks of overstocking and stockouts, allowing companies to meet customer demand even during disruptions.

Improved Customer Satisfaction:

In today's customer-centric market, maintaining high service levels is crucial for competitiveness. Stockouts or delays in fulfilling orders can lead to lost sales, damage to brand reputation, and decreased customer loyalty.

A demand-driven approach helps companies maintain optimal inventory levels, ensuring that products are available when customers need them. This responsiveness enhances customer satisfaction and supports long-term brand loyalty.

Cost Efficiency:

Traditional inventory management often leads to excessive stock levels, resulting in high carrying costs, waste, and markdowns. Overstocking not only ties up capital but also increases storage and handling expenses.

Demand-driven inventory management reduces the need for high safety stock levels by aligning inventory with actual demand. This leads to lower carrying costs, reduced waste, and improved cash flow, contributing to greater cost efficiency.

Better Management of Supply Chain Disruptions:

Recent global events, such as the COVID-19 pandemic and geopolitical tensions, have highlighted the vulnerability of supply chains to disruption. Companies that rely on traditional inventory models may find themselves unprepared for sudden supply chain shocks.

Demand-driven inventory management provides a resilient framework, allowing companies to react quickly to disruptions by adjusting inventory levels in response to real-time data. This adaptability helps companies mitigate the impact of supply chain interruptions and maintain continuity of supply.

Enhanced Decision-Making through Data:

A demand-driven approach relies on data analytics and real-time insights, empowering decision-makers with a more accurate understanding of demand patterns. This data-driven perspective enables better planning and forecasting, making inventory decisions more informed and strategic.

Advanced technologies like AI and machine learning, often incorporated into demand-driven systems, further enhance predictive capabilities. These tools provide actionable insights, allowing businesses to optimize inventory levels, improve forecasting accuracy, and anticipate future demand trends.

Alignment with Modern Business Strategies:

Many companies are embracing lean and agile methodologies to increase efficiency and reduce waste. Demand-driven inventory management aligns well with these modern business strategies, as it promotes just-in-time (JIT) inventory practices and minimizes excess stock.

Furthermore, demand-driven models support sustainability goals by reducing waste and excess production. This approach aligns with the growing consumer demand for environmentally responsible business practices, making it an attractive option for companies looking to enhance their sustainability initiatives.

Competitive Advantage:

In a demand-driven marketplace, speed and accuracy are key differentiators. Companies that adopt demand-driven inventory practices gain a competitive edge by being able to respond to market changes faster than their competitors.

By reducing lead times, enhancing customer service, and lowering inventory costs, demand-driven companies position themselves as agile market leaders. This competitive advantage can lead to increased market share, improved brand reputation, and greater profitability.

In conclusion, demand-driven inventory management offers a robust framework for companies looking to thrive in today's challenging market environment. By focusing on real-time demand, responsive replenishment, and data-driven decision-making, this approach enables organizations to manage inventory more effectively, reduce costs, and improve customer satisfaction. As global supply chains continue to evolve, demand-driven inventory management will play an increasingly critical role in helping companies remain resilient and adaptable in the face of uncertainty.

Chapter 2: The Role of Inventory in the Supply Chain

Effective inventory management is one of the most crucial elements of a well-functioning supply chain. Inventory represents a significant portion of a company's assets and is central to its ability to meet customer demand, manage costs, and maintain operational efficiency. This chapter explores the purpose and strategic role of inventory in the supply chain, different types of inventory, and how inventory management influences both efficiency and cost structures.

Purpose of Inventory within the Supply Chain

Inventory serves several critical functions within a supply chain, each contributing to the ability to meet demand and maintain the flow of goods from suppliers to customers. The main purposes of holding inventory in a supply chain include:

Buffer Against Demand Variability:

Inventory acts as a buffer against fluctuations in customer demand. Having stock on hand enables companies to fulfill orders even when demand exceeds forecasts or fluctuates unexpectedly. This reduces the risk of stockouts and lost sales, ensuring customers receive products when needed.

Enabling Production Efficiency:

By holding raw materials and work-in-progress (WIP) inventory, companies can ensure that their production lines operate smoothly and efficiently. This prevents production delays that could arise from waiting for materials and helps maintain a steady flow of goods through the production process.

Supporting Lead Times:

Lead times are inherent in any supply chain due to sourcing, production, and transportation delays. Inventory allows companies to bridge the time gap between ordering materials, producing goods, and delivering finished products to customers. This ensures that demand can be met even while goods are in transit or production stages.

Mitigating Supply Chain Risks:

Inventory can serve as a hedge against risks associated with supply disruptions. For example, disruptions in global supply chains caused by events like natural disasters, political unrest, or supplier failures can impact material availability. Strategic inventory levels help companies continue operations despite these risks.

Facilitating Economies of Scale:

Inventory enables companies to take advantage of bulk purchasing discounts and production economies of scale. By buying in larger quantities, companies can reduce per-unit costs, benefiting from lower purchasing and transportation expenses.

Providing Seasonal and Market Flexibility:

Many industries experience seasonal demand patterns, and inventory allows companies to stock up in anticipation of peak seasons or adjust to slow periods. Additionally, companies can stock inventory to respond to promotional activities, new product launches, or market-specific demands.

In summary, inventory serves as a strategic tool for managing demand, buffering against disruptions, and supporting production and market requirements. However, while inventory provides essential benefits, holding excessive or unnecessary inventory can lead to significant costs. Therefore, effective inventory management is essential for balancing availability and cost.

Types of Inventory: Raw Materials, Work-In-Progress, and Finished Goods

Understanding the types of inventory within a supply chain is essential for optimizing management strategies. Broadly, inventory can be

15

categorized into three main types, each serving a different purpose within the supply chain:

Raw Materials Inventory:

Raw materials are the unprocessed resources used in manufacturing finished products. These materials are typically purchased from suppliers and kept in storage until they are needed in production. For example, in a furniture manufacturing company, wood, metal, and paint would be classified as raw materials.

Raw materials inventory is essential for ensuring production continuity. If raw materials are not readily available, production halts, leading to delays in fulfilling customer orders and potential losses. Effective management of raw materials inventory involves balancing supply availability with demand to avoid stockouts without over-investing in unnecessary materials.

Work-In-Progress (WIP) Inventory:

Work-in-progress (WIP) inventory refers to partially finished goods that are still in various stages of production. For instance, in an automotive plant, a partially assembled car represents WIP inventory until it reaches the final assembly stage.

WIP inventory serves to keep the production process moving smoothly, but excessive WIP can lead to inefficiencies, increased holding costs, and complications in tracking items through production. Proper WIP management involves streamlining production stages to minimize idle inventory while maintaining a continuous workflow.

Finished Goods Inventory:

Finished goods are completed products that are ready for sale or distribution to customers. For a retailer, finished goods are the inventory displayed on shelves or stored in a warehouse awaiting customer orders.

Finished goods inventory is crucial for meeting customer demand promptly, ensuring products are available when needed. However, excessive finished goods inventory can tie up capital and lead to issues such as obsolescence, especially in industries where products have a limited shelf life or rapidly changing trends.

Additional types of inventory may include maintenance, repair, and operations (MRO) items (e.g., spare parts, tools, and office supplies) that support ongoing operations, and safety stock, which is additional inventory held as a buffer against demand or supply uncertainties. Each inventory type requires tailored management strategies to minimize costs while ensuring operational continuity and customer satisfaction.

How Inventory Management Impacts Efficiency and Costs

Inventory management plays a central role in optimizing supply chain performance by balancing the need for product availability with the cost implications of holding inventory. The efficiency of a supply chain often hinges on effective inventory management practices, as well-managed inventory helps control costs, improves customer service, and supports smooth production flows. Key ways in which inventory management impacts efficiency and costs include:

Inventory Carrying Costs:

Inventory carrying costs refer to the total cost of holding inventory, including warehousing, insurance, depreciation, and opportunity costs. The longer inventory is held, the more these costs accumulate, impacting a company's profitability.

Effective inventory management minimizes carrying costs by reducing excess stock, implementing just-in-time (JIT) practices, and improving turnover rates. For example, by aligning inventory levels with real-time demand, companies can reduce the space and resources required to store excess inventory.

Stockout and Lost Sales Costs:

Stockouts occur when a company runs out of inventory needed to fulfill customer orders. This leads to lost sales, dissatisfied customers, and potentially damaged brand reputation.

Inventory management practices such as demand forecasting, safety stock calculation, and responsive replenishment reduce the risk of stockouts. By accurately predicting demand and adjusting inventory levels accordingly, companies can enhance customer satisfaction and maintain service levels.

Order and Setup Costs:

Ordering and setup costs arise every time new inventory is ordered or manufactured. These costs include purchase order processing, transportation, and setup of machinery for new production runs. For example, smaller, frequent orders may reduce carrying costs but increase order costs.

Inventory management helps balance order and setup costs by optimizing reorder points and order quantities. Economic order quantity (EOQ) models, for instance, calculate the ideal order quantity to minimize combined holding and ordering costs, supporting cost-effective inventory management.

Production and Operational Efficiency:

Efficient inventory management ensures that raw materials and components are available for production when needed, minimizing delays and downtime. By having the right inventory on hand, companies can maintain a steady production flow and reduce idle time.

Properly managed WIP and finished goods inventory also streamline production cycles and warehouse operations. Lean inventory practices, such as kanban systems, support JIT production, allowing companies to produce only what is needed, reducing waste, and improving efficiency.

Lead Times and Flexibility:

Effective inventory management improves lead times by ensuring that products are readily available for customer orders. By reducing lead times, companies can fulfill customer orders faster, improving responsiveness to market demands.

Inventory management that incorporates demand-driven practices increases flexibility, allowing companies to adapt to sudden demand changes or supply disruptions. This agility is critical in today's volatile markets, where customer expectations for fast delivery are higher than ever.

Cash Flow and Working Capital:

Inventory ties up working capital that could otherwise be used for other business investments. Excessive inventory strains cash flow, reducing the funds available for innovation, expansion, or other revenue-generating activities.

Inventory management practices such as reducing excess stock, increasing inventory turnover, and implementing JIT systems free up cash, improving liquidity and financial health. Companies that optimize their inventory have greater financial flexibility and can allocate resources more effectively.

Sustainability and Waste Reduction:

Poorly managed inventory can lead to waste due to obsolescence, spoilage, or damage, which is particularly relevant for industries handling perishable goods or products with short life cycles.

Inventory management helps reduce waste by implementing turnover practices and demand-driven inventory strategies that match supply with demand more accurately. By reducing unnecessary production and storage, companies minimize their environmental footprint, aligning inventory practices with sustainability goals.

In conclusion, inventory management is a fundamental component of supply chain efficiency and cost control. By strategically managing raw materials, WIP, and finished goods, companies can ensure smooth production, meet customer demand, and reduce operational costs. Through efficient inventory practices, businesses can enhance responsiveness, maintain service levels, and gain a competitive edge in the market. As global supply chains become increasingly complex, effective inventory management will remain essential for driving both profitability and sustainability.

Chapter 3: Core Concepts of Demand-Driven Inventory

Demand-driven inventory management has emerged as a response to the increasing complexity and unpredictability of modern supply chains. Traditional inventory systems, which often rely on historical data and forecast-based replenishment, may fail to meet the needs of businesses operating in volatile and customer-driven markets. This chapter introduces the core concepts of demand-driven inventory management, exploring the key principles behind this approach, the benefits of aligning inventory with demand patterns, and a foundational methodology known as Demand-Driven Material Requirements Planning (DDMRP).

Key Principles: Pull-Based Systems and Real-Time Demand Data

The demand-driven inventory approach is built on two foundational principles that differentiate it from traditional models: pull-based systems and the use of real-time demand data.

Pull-Based Systems:

In traditional inventory systems, the "push" approach is commonly used, where goods are manufactured or ordered based on demand forecasts. These forecasts, however, can be inaccurate, leading to overstocking or stockouts. The pull-based system, by contrast, prioritizes producing or replenishing inventory only when actual customer demand exists.

Pull-based inventory systems are demand-driven, meaning that replenishment decisions are made in response to real customer orders rather than projections. This shift reduces the risk of holding excess inventory and enables companies to be more responsive to customer needs.

The pull-based principle was initially popularized by lean manufacturing methodologies, such as the Toyota Production System, and has since been adapted across various industries. This approach minimizes waste, reduces lead times, and enables companies to remain agile in a rapidly changing environment.

Real-Time Demand Data:

Real-time data provides companies with up-to-the-minute insights into customer orders, market trends, and inventory levels. By leveraging digital tools like the Internet of Things (IoT), cloud computing, and advanced analytics, companies can gather and analyze demand data as it occurs.

Access to real-time demand data allows companies to make immediate and informed decisions regarding inventory replenishment, production schedules, and logistics. This minimizes the reliance on static, historical forecasts and enhances a company's ability to adapt to sudden changes in demand or supply conditions.

Real-time data facilitates a more accurate demand signal, reducing the need for safety stock and enabling better alignment between inventory levels and customer demand. It also helps companies identify patterns and seasonal variations, which can be integrated into inventory planning for more strategic decision-making.

By adhering to pull-based systems and real-time demand data, demand-driven inventory management allows companies to be more responsive, adaptive, and efficient. These principles enable businesses to reduce excess inventory, enhance service levels, and improve cash flow by aligning inventory levels with actual customer needs.

Benefits of Aligning Inventory with Demand Patterns

Aligning inventory with demand patterns brings several benefits that contribute to a more resilient and efficient supply chain. Some of the key advantages include:

Reduced Inventory Costs:

By aligning inventory with real-time demand, companies can avoid the costly problem of overstocking, which leads to high carrying costs, storage expenses, and potential obsolescence. A demand-driven approach allows companies to maintain leaner inventory levels, reducing warehousing needs and freeing up capital.

When inventory levels are optimized based on actual demand, companies can reduce the financial impact of unsold stock and avoid markdowns, write-offs, or wastage that arise from holding excess inventory.

Improved Service Levels and Customer Satisfaction:

A demand-driven approach enables companies to better meet customer expectations by ensuring that products are available when and where they are needed. By responding directly to demand, companies can reduce stockouts and backorders, improving on-time delivery rates and customer satisfaction.

In today's competitive landscape, customer satisfaction is closely tied to a company's ability to fulfill orders quickly and accurately. Aligning inventory with demand patterns supports faster order fulfillment, boosting customer loyalty and enhancing brand reputation.

Enhanced Agility and Responsiveness:

Demand-driven inventory management provides companies with the flexibility to respond to shifts in demand more effectively. In contrast to traditional models that rely on forecast-based production and ordering, a demand-driven approach empowers businesses to adapt quickly to changes in customer preferences, seasonality, or market conditions.

This agility is particularly valuable in industries with short product life cycles or high variability in demand, such as technology, fashion, and consumer electronics. With a demand-driven approach, companies can adjust their inventory levels more frequently, reducing the risk of obsolescence and enhancing adaptability to market trends.

Better Cash Flow and Working Capital Management:

Excess inventory ties up working capital that could otherwise be invested in growth initiatives, innovation, or customer service improvements. By aligning inventory with demand, companies can reduce excess stock, minimize waste, and improve cash flow.

Demand-driven inventory management promotes efficient use of resources, ensuring that inventory investments align with actual customer needs. This enables businesses to allocate their capital more effectively, supporting financial stability and long-term growth.

Reduced Lead Times and Faster Replenishment:

In a demand-driven model, companies optimize inventory replenishment based on real-time demand signals, resulting in shorter lead times and faster order cycles. By reducing unnecessary inventory steps, companies can respond to demand surges without delay, enhancing customer satisfaction and competitive positioning.

Faster replenishment also reduces the need for safety stock, as companies can restock inventory in response to actual orders rather than relying solely on forecasts. This minimizes the holding of excess inventory and contributes to leaner, more efficient operations.

In summary, aligning inventory with demand patterns allows companies to achieve a balance between service levels and inventory costs, providing them with the flexibility to respond to changing market conditions. By focusing on actual demand, companies can reduce inventory waste, improve customer satisfaction, and enhance operational efficiency.

Demand-Driven Material Requirements Planning (DDMRP) Overview

Demand-Driven Material Requirements Planning (DDMRP) is a modern inventory management methodology that builds on the principles of demand-driven inventory management. Developed by Carol Ptak and Chad Smith, DDMRP is designed to address the limitations of traditional Material Requirements Planning (MRP) systems in today's fast-paced and customer-driven markets. DDMRP integrates key demand-driven concepts into a structured approach to inventory management and production planning.

Overview of Traditional MRP Systems:

Traditional MRP systems were developed to schedule production based on forecasted demand and Bill of Materials (BOM) data. While these systems provide a systematic approach to planning, they are heavily reliant on forecasts, making them vulnerable to inaccuracies and demand fluctuations.

Traditional MRP systems often use "push" logic, where products are manufactured based on forecasted demand rather than actual orders. This can result in either excessive inventory or shortages, as production is not directly aligned with real-time customer needs.

Core Components of DDMRP:

Strategic Inventory Positioning: DDMRP emphasizes placing inventory in specific locations within the supply chain where it can provide the greatest benefit in terms of buffering against demand variability. This positioning enables companies to maintain an optimal inventory level while responding to demand shifts.

Buffer Profiles and Levels: In DDMRP, inventory buffers are established to act as shock absorbers, allowing for more flexible response to demand fluctuations. Buffers are categorized based on demand patterns, lead times, and variability, and are managed dynamically to reflect changing conditions.

Dynamic Adjustments: DDMRP uses real-time data to adjust buffer levels as demand patterns change. By continuously monitoring and adjusting buffers, companies can maintain appropriate inventory levels, reduce stockouts, and prevent overstocking.

Demand-Driven Planning: Unlike traditional MRP, which relies on forecast-driven schedules, DDMRP uses actual demand signals to guide production and replenishment decisions. This demand-driven approach ensures that production and ordering are closely aligned with current market demand, reducing waste and enhancing responsiveness.

Execution Tools: DDMRP provides execution tools that enable companies to prioritize orders based on buffer status and demand urgency. This ensures that critical customer orders are fulfilled on time, even when inventory is low or demand spikes.

Advantages of DDMRP:

Enhanced Responsiveness: By focusing on actual demand signals rather than forecasts, DDMRP allows companies to respond more quickly to changes in customer orders, minimizing lead times and improving customer satisfaction.

Reduced Inventory Levels: DDMRP's dynamic buffer management reduces the need for excessive safety stock, leading to leaner inventory levels and lower carrying costs.

Increased Supply Chain Visibility: The structured approach of DDMRP enables better visibility into inventory levels and demand patterns across the supply chain. This supports data-driven decision-making and enables proactive inventory management.

Alignment with Modern Supply Chain Needs: In fast-paced markets, where product life cycles are short and customer expectations are high, DDMRP provides the agility and adaptability that traditional MRP systems often lack.

DDMRP offers companies a framework for achieving demand-driven inventory management, balancing inventory levels, and aligning production with real-time demand signals. It allows companies to achieve the responsiveness and cost-efficiency required in today's competitive landscape.

In conclusion, demand-driven inventory management represents a significant shift from traditional inventory models. By focusing on pull-based systems and real-time demand data, this approach enables companies to reduce excess inventory, respond to market changes with agility, and better meet customer expectations. DDMRP offers a structured methodology for implementing demand-driven principles, aligning inventory levels with actual demand patterns, and enhancing supply chain responsiveness.

Chapter 4: Understanding Demand Forecasting

Demand forecasting is a critical component of inventory management, serving as the foundation upon which many supply chain decisions are based. Accurately predicting customer demand helps businesses optimize inventory levels, avoid stockouts and overstock situations, and improve operational efficiency. This chapter delves into the importance of accurate demand forecasting, introduces common techniques and tools used in forecasting, and discusses how forecast accuracy directly impacts inventory levels.

Importance of Accurate Demand Forecasting

Demand forecasting is a key driver of effective inventory management, helping businesses anticipate future demand, streamline production schedules, and optimize order fulfillment. By understanding future demand, companies can better align their resources with market needs, reducing costs and increasing responsiveness. Here are several reasons why accurate demand forecasting is essential:

Optimizing Inventory Levels:

Forecasting helps companies maintain the right inventory balance by predicting future demand for each product. By accurately forecasting demand, businesses can reduce excess inventory, minimize storage costs, and avoid the pitfalls of overstocking or stockouts.

Proper inventory levels ensure that businesses have enough stock on hand to meet customer demands without tying up unnecessary capital in unsold goods.

Improving Customer Satisfaction:

Demand forecasting allows businesses to anticipate when and where products will be needed, reducing the likelihood of stockouts that could disrupt customer satisfaction. By ensuring that products are available at the right time, businesses can improve on-time delivery rates and strengthen customer loyalty.

High forecast accuracy directly contributes to better order fulfillment rates, shorter lead times, and improved customer satisfaction, all of which are crucial in today's competitive market.

Enhancing Operational Efficiency:

Forecasting enables companies to plan their production, procurement, and distribution processes more effectively. By aligning resources with anticipated demand, businesses can optimize production schedules, reduce waste, and improve overall operational efficiency.

Accurate forecasts allow for streamlined procurement, where raw materials are purchased in sync with production needs, avoiding excessive storage costs and improving cash flow.

Reducing Costs and Managing Risks:

Overproduction, obsolescence, and high holding costs are risks associated with inaccurate forecasting. By predicting demand more accurately, companies can reduce these risks, lowering costs associated with inventory, warehousing, and unsold products.

Effective forecasting minimizes the financial risks of unsold inventory or emergency restocking. It also allows companies to adjust to changes in market conditions, such as seasonal demand variations or shifts in consumer preferences.

Supporting Strategic Decision-Making:

Demand forecasting provides data-driven insights that support strategic decisions, such as product launches, promotional campaigns, and expansion into new markets. Accurate forecasts enable managers to make informed choices about resource allocation, marketing investments, and supply chain adjustments.

Accurate demand forecasting is the cornerstone of demand-driven inventory management, enabling businesses to align inventory levels with customer needs and market fluctuations.

Techniques and Tools for Forecasting

There are several forecasting methods available, ranging from simple to complex models. Choosing the right forecasting technique depends on factors such as the data available, the nature of demand, and the level of accuracy required. Below are two primary categories of forecasting techniques: time series models and causal models.

Time Series Models:

Time series models are based on historical data and identify patterns or trends that are likely to continue in the future. These models are particularly useful for products with consistent demand patterns over time.

Some commonly used time series forecasting techniques include:

Moving Averages:

Moving averages smooth out short-term fluctuations by calculating the average of a specified number of past periods. This technique is simple and easy to apply, making it suitable for stable demand patterns with little variability.

By taking an average of recent data points, moving averages provide a clear trend direction, though they may lag behind actual trends if demand changes rapidly.

Exponential Smoothing:

Exponential smoothing assigns exponentially decreasing weights to past observations, giving more importance to recent data. Variants such as simple exponential smoothing, double exponential smoothing (for trends), and triple exponential smoothing (for seasonality) allow businesses to forecast demand that includes trends and seasonality.

This technique is more responsive to recent changes in demand patterns, making it suitable for moderately volatile products.

Seasonal Decomposition of Time Series (STL):

STL decomposes time series data into trend, seasonal, and residual components. This approach is helpful for forecasting products with seasonal demand variations, such as holiday-related items or products affected by weather conditions.

By identifying seasonal cycles, companies can prepare for predictable fluctuations, ensuring inventory availability during peak periods and avoiding overstocking during low-demand seasons.

ARIMA (Auto-Regressive Integrated Moving Average):

ARIMA is a more sophisticated time series model that combines autoregressive and moving average techniques, allowing it to account for trends, seasonality, and irregular patterns in demand data.

This model is particularly effective for longer-term forecasting when historical data is abundant and demand patterns exhibit complexity beyond simple trends and seasonality.

Causal Models:

Causal models, also known as explanatory models, assume that demand is influenced by specific external factors, such as economic indicators, promotional activities, or weather conditions. These models attempt to identify the causal relationship between demand and influencing variables.

Common causal forecasting techniques include:

Regression Analysis:

Regression analysis examines the relationship between dependent and independent variables to forecast demand. For example, a retailer might use historical sales data and advertising spending to predict future sales.

Linear regression is a basic form of this analysis, while multiple regression models can include various factors, providing a more comprehensive view of demand influences.

Econometric Models:

Econometric models are complex mathematical representations that consider various macroeconomic factors, such as interest rates, unemployment, or consumer spending, to forecast demand.

These models are often used for industries sensitive to economic cycles, such as automotive or real estate, and can provide insights into long-term demand trends.

Machine Learning and Artificial Intelligence (AI):

Advanced machine learning algorithms, including neural networks and random forests, are increasingly used in demand forecasting. These algorithms can analyze large datasets, identifying hidden patterns and making highly accurate predictions, especially for products with complex demand patterns.

AI-based models can incorporate a variety of data sources, from transactional data to external market indicators, improving accuracy over traditional methods.

Forecast Accuracy and Its Impact on Inventory Levels

Forecast accuracy is critical for inventory management, as it directly influences decisions regarding replenishment, production scheduling, and inventory levels. The closer a forecast is to actual demand, the fewer adjustments are required, resulting in a more efficient supply chain. Inaccurate forecasts, on the other hand, can lead to costly inefficiencies, either from holding too much stock or from frequent stockouts. Here's how forecast accuracy impacts inventory levels:

Reducing Safety Stock Requirements:

Forecast accuracy reduces the need for large safety stock buffers, which are typically used to protect against uncertainty in demand. With more precise forecasts, companies can maintain leaner inventories, freeing up capital and reducing carrying costs.

High forecast accuracy leads to a more efficient allocation of safety stock, allowing companies to allocate resources to products that truly need them.

Improving Service Levels:

Accurate forecasts enable businesses to meet customer demand consistently, reducing stockouts and backorders. This directly improves service levels, as companies can fulfill orders promptly, reducing the risk of customer dissatisfaction.

Better service levels are a competitive advantage, particularly in markets where timely delivery is a key differentiator.

Minimizing Excess Inventory:

Excess inventory is often a result of overestimating demand. Holding too much stock ties up working capital, increases storage costs, and can lead to product obsolescence. By improving forecast accuracy, companies can avoid overproduction and excess inventory, optimizing storage space and reducing waste.

With more accurate demand data, companies can focus on products with consistent demand, limiting inventory risks associated with slow-moving items.

Enhancing Responsiveness to Demand Fluctuations:

Accurate forecasting improves a company's ability to adjust to unexpected changes in demand. For instance, if an unexpected surge occurs, precise forecasting can signal the need to increase production or expedite orders, reducing the risk of lost sales.

In a demand-driven environment, responsiveness to fluctuations is essential for meeting customer expectations and minimizing lost revenue.

Impact on Production Planning and Procurement:

Forecast accuracy helps align production schedules and procurement with actual demand. This alignment minimizes the risk of material shortages or production delays, enhancing overall efficiency in manufacturing and supplier management.

For companies with extensive lead times, accurate forecasts enable better planning, reducing the need for rush orders, which are often more costly and less reliable.

In summary, understanding demand forecasting is essential for effective inventory management in a demand-driven approach. Accurate forecasting enables companies to anticipate demand patterns, optimize inventory levels, and improve responsiveness. By selecting the appropriate forecasting techniques, such as time series or causal models, and focusing on accuracy, businesses can reduce costs, enhance customer satisfaction, and achieve a competitive advantage in the marketplace. Demand forecasting, therefore, is a vital component of demand-driven inventory management, aligning inventory with market needs and supporting a responsive, agile supply chain.

Chapter 5: Inventory Positioning and Buffer Strategies

Effective inventory positioning and buffer management are crucial for aligning stock levels with demand fluctuations, minimizing risks associated with lead time variability, and ensuring high service levels. This chapter explores how to determine optimal inventory locations within the supply chain, strategies for buffering against demand volatility, and best practices for maintaining buffer stock.

Determining Optimal Inventory Locations Within the Supply Chain

Proper inventory positioning is essential to ensure products are available when and where they are needed. It requires careful analysis of demand patterns, customer locations, transportation costs, and lead times. Determining the right inventory placement can streamline logistics, reduce delivery times, and minimize overall costs. Here are some key considerations when determining optimal inventory locations:

Demand Centers and Customer Proximity:

Locating inventory close to primary demand centers or customer hubs reduces transit times, allowing faster order fulfillment. By analyzing geographic demand data, companies can identify locations where inventory is most likely to be needed and prioritize these areas for stocking.

For instance, e-commerce businesses often place distribution centers near major urban areas to expedite last-mile delivery and enhance service levels.

Lead Times and Supply Reliability:

Understanding lead time variability is essential in positioning inventory. When lead times are predictable and short, companies may not need as many distribution centers. However, in cases where lead times are longer or variable, positioning inventory closer to demand locations helps mitigate delays.

In industries like automotive, where parts must arrive just-in-time, strategically placed inventory closer to manufacturing plants or assembly lines can reduce production delays caused by late shipments.

Cost Optimization:

Inventory positioning decisions must balance the costs of warehousing and transportation. A centralized inventory location reduces warehousing costs but may increase shipping expenses and lead times. Conversely, a decentralized approach with multiple inventory locations close to demand areas reduces shipping costs and lead times but increases warehousing expenses.

Many companies use a hybrid model, combining central warehouses for bulk storage with regional hubs for faster distribution, optimizing both costs and service levels.

Risk Management and Flexibility:

Positioning inventory strategically across multiple locations mitigates risks associated with supply chain disruptions, such as natural disasters or geopolitical events. By diversifying inventory across regions, companies reduce the impact of localized disruptions.

Additionally, multi-location positioning provides greater flexibility to reallocate inventory in response to sudden demand shifts, supporting an agile supply chain.

Inventory Visibility and Technology Integration:

Advanced technology solutions, such as warehouse management systems (WMS) and inventory tracking tools, enhance visibility across inventory locations. This allows companies to monitor stock levels in real-time, improving replenishment accuracy and enabling proactive decision-making.

Data-driven insights from these systems guide inventory positioning decisions, ensuring that high-demand areas have adequate stock while low-demand areas are not overstocked.

By analyzing demand, lead times, costs, and risks, businesses can strategically position inventory to optimize availability, minimize costs, and enhance responsiveness to customer needs.

Buffering for Demand Volatility and Lead Time Variability

Buffering is a strategy for managing uncertainty by holding additional inventory to cover fluctuations in demand or lead times. This helps prevent stockouts and maintains service levels even in unpredictable circumstances. Two key areas for which buffering is necessary include demand volatility and lead time variability.

Buffering for Demand Volatility:

Demand volatility refers to sudden or unexpected changes in customer demand. This could be due to seasonal trends, market trends, promotional events, or other unpredictable factors. Buffer stock acts as a cushion, enabling businesses to meet unexpected spikes in demand without delays.

In consumer-driven markets, demand volatility is high, especially during holidays or peak seasons. Companies often forecast potential demand spikes and build buffer stock accordingly to handle these peaks.

Buffering for Lead Time Variability:

Lead time variability arises from inconsistencies in the time it takes suppliers to deliver goods, which can be affected by factors such as shipping delays, supplier issues, or logistical disruptions. Lead time buffering helps ensure inventory is available even when there are unexpected supply chain delays.

For products with long or variable lead times, holding safety stock is essential to maintain uninterrupted operations. This buffer reduces reliance on immediate supplier deliveries, offering a backup for smooth production and order fulfillment.

Techniques for Determining Buffer Levels:

Safety Stock Calculations: Companies often use statistical methods to determine optimal safety stock levels based on demand and lead time variability. Common approaches include calculating safety stock as a function of service level targets, standard deviations in demand, and lead time.

Demand-Driven MRP (DDMRP): DDMRP is an approach that incorporates buffer positioning and levels directly into material requirements planning, allowing companies to hold the appropriate amount of buffer stock based on real-time demand signals and dynamic adjustments.

Inventory Modeling and Simulation: Advanced modeling techniques, such as Monte Carlo simulations, help companies simulate various demand and supply scenarios, allowing them to adjust buffer levels based on potential outcomes and risks.

Buffering strategies enable companies to protect against demand and supply uncertainties, ensuring continuity in supply chain operations even under volatile conditions.

Strategies for Maintaining Buffer Stock

Maintaining buffer stock involves carefully balancing the need to prevent stockouts with the desire to avoid excessive inventory. The following strategies help companies achieve optimal buffer levels without tying up too much capital in excess stock:

Establishing Service Level Targets:

Service level targets define the percentage of customer demand that should be met without stockouts. Higher service level targets require more buffer stock, while lower targets allow for leaner buffers. Companies typically set service levels based on customer expectations, industry standards, and cost considerations.

For example, a 95% service level means the business aims to meet 95% of demand from available stock, while accepting that 5% may experience delays. Balancing service level goals with buffer stock levels is crucial for efficient inventory management.

Dynamic Buffer Adjustments:

Traditional static buffers may not effectively respond to changes in demand or lead times. Implementing a dynamic buffer approach allows companies to adjust buffer stock levels based on real-time demand data and trends, preventing overstock or understock situations.

Demand-driven inventory management systems, like DDMRP, use demand signals to adjust buffer levels, making the approach more responsive to actual market needs.

Segmentation of Inventory:

Not all products require the same level of buffering. By segmenting inventory based on factors like demand variability, value, and criticality, companies can allocate buffer stock more efficiently. High-demand, high-variability items might require larger buffers, while stable, low-demand products can be stocked leaner.

ABC analysis, which classifies items into categories based on their importance, helps companies prioritize buffering resources for high-impact items, maximizing the cost-effectiveness of buffer stock investments.

Utilizing Supplier Partnerships:

Collaborating closely with suppliers can reduce the need for high buffer stock levels. For example, suppliers that offer shorter lead times or flexible delivery schedules allow businesses to maintain lower buffers while still meeting demand.

Strong supplier relationships may also provide access to vendor-managed inventory (VMI) arrangements, in which suppliers monitor and replenish stock, ensuring optimal buffer levels without requiring additional storage.

Continuous Review and Optimization:

Buffer stock requirements change over time due to shifts in demand patterns, market conditions, and supply chain dynamics. Regularly reviewing and adjusting buffer levels is essential for maintaining an efficient inventory system.

Inventory management software that tracks demand trends, lead times, and stock levels allows companies to continuously monitor buffer effectiveness, adjusting as needed to balance availability and costs.

In summary, inventory positioning and buffer strategies are critical elements of demand-driven inventory management. By strategically determining inventory locations, buffering for demand and lead time variability, and implementing effective buffer stock maintenance strategies, companies can achieve a responsive, efficient, and resilient supply chain. With a strong understanding of these concepts, businesses can better manage risk, reduce costs, and meet customer demands in an ever-changing marketplace.

Chapter 6: Setting Inventory Policies and Targets

Inventory policies and targets form the backbone of an effective demand-driven inventory management system. They help in setting guidelines for when and how much inventory to order, ensuring that companies can meet customer demands while controlling inventory costs. In this chapter, we will explore various types of inventory policies, including continuous and periodic review systems, as well as the process of establishing reorder points, safety stocks, and order quantities. Lastly, we'll discuss how to balance service levels and inventory costs to achieve an optimal inventory management strategy.

Types of Inventory Policies: Continuous Review and Periodic Review

Inventory policies define the rules for monitoring stock levels, determining when to reorder, and managing stock to avoid shortages or overstock situations. The two primary types of inventory review policies—continuous review and periodic review—each have their unique advantages and applications in different business contexts.

Continuous Review (Q-System):

In a continuous review system, inventory levels are continuously monitored, and an order is placed whenever stock reaches a predetermined reorder point (ROP). This system is ideal for items with high demand volatility or critical stock that requires consistent availability.

Advantages: Continuous review provides real-time visibility and helps prevent stockouts, as the system triggers a reorder as soon as inventory reaches the ROP. It is particularly useful for high-value or fast-moving items where frequent stockouts could lead to lost sales or customer dissatisfaction.

Applications: Continuous review is commonly used in industries with fluctuating demand or when managing high-priority stock. For

45

instance, medical supplies or perishable goods benefit from this system as they often require precise inventory control.

Technology Requirements: To successfully implement continuous review, businesses often need automated inventory management systems that can monitor stock levels in real-time and generate alerts or orders as soon as inventory falls to the reorder point.

Periodic Review (P-System):

In a periodic review system, inventory levels are checked at regular intervals (e.g., weekly, biweekly, or monthly). Orders are placed at the end of each review period to bring inventory up to a predetermined target level. This approach works well for products with stable demand and for companies that prefer to consolidate orders to reduce administrative workload.

Advantages: Periodic review systems reduce the need for constant monitoring and are useful for items with predictable demand. They also allow businesses to consolidate orders, which can reduce shipping costs and improve supplier relationships.

Applications: Industries with consistent, predictable demand (e.g., consumer goods or retail sectors) often use periodic review systems. For instance, items with regular replenishment schedules, such as office supplies, benefit from periodic review due to their stable demand patterns.

Inventory Variance: While periodic review may lead to greater variability in inventory levels, setting an appropriate target level at each review period can help mitigate this issue.

Selecting the right inventory policy depends on factors such as demand patterns, product value, and inventory management goals. Many companies use a hybrid approach, employing continuous review for critical or high-value items while managing less critical items under a periodic review system.

Establishing Reorder Points, Safety Stocks, and Order Quantities

Setting appropriate reorder points, safety stocks, and order quantities is essential for maintaining efficient inventory levels. Each of these components plays a distinct role in ensuring that inventory is replenished in a timely manner without tying up excessive capital in stock.

Reorder Point (ROP):

The reorder point is the inventory level at which a new order is triggered to avoid running out of stock. It accounts for lead time (the time it takes for an order to arrive after it is placed) and demand during that lead time.

Calculation: ROP is typically calculated as the product of average demand during lead time. For example, if a company sells 10 units per day and the lead time is five days, the ROP would be 50 units.

Dynamic Adjustments: In demand-driven environments, reorder points are sometimes dynamically adjusted based on demand trends or seasonality. For instance, companies may set higher reorder points during peak seasons to accommodate increased demand.

Safety Stock:

Safety stock serves as a buffer against demand or supply variability. It helps ensure that stock is available to cover unexpected spikes in demand or delays in supply. Calculating safety stock requires analyzing demand variability and lead time.

Safety Stock Calculation: Many companies calculate safety stock using statistical methods, considering the standard deviation of demand and lead time variability. A common formula is:

Safety Stock

$$\text{Safety Stock} = Z \times \sigma(\text{demand}) \times \sqrt{\text{lead time}}$$

where

Z

Z is the service level factor based on the desired service level.

Setting Service Levels: Safety stock levels depend on the company's service level targets. Higher service levels require more safety stock, but they also increase holding costs. Balancing service level requirements with inventory costs is crucial for optimal stock management.

Order Quantities:

Order quantity is the amount of inventory ordered at each replenishment point. Determining the optimal order quantity requires balancing order costs with holding costs to minimize total inventory costs.

Economic Order Quantity (EOQ): EOQ is a popular formula used to determine the ideal order quantity that minimizes total inventory costs. The EOQ formula is:

EOQ

$$\text{EOQ} = \sqrt{\frac{2DS}{H}}$$

Adjusting EOQ for Demand Variability: For items with highly variable demand, EOQ may need to be adjusted to account for fluctuations. In these cases, companies may combine EOQ with reorder point strategies or implement dynamic ordering policies.

Setting reorder points, safety stock, and order quantities helps companies maintain balanced inventory levels, minimizing the risk of stockouts while avoiding excessive holding costs.

Balancing Service Levels and Inventory Costs

Balancing service levels with inventory costs is a critical aspect of setting inventory policies. High service levels improve customer satisfaction by reducing stockouts, but they also increase inventory costs. Achieving the right balance is key to maintaining a cost-effective inventory system.

Determining Service Levels:

Service levels represent the percentage of customer demand that should be met without a stockout. Higher service levels require more safety stock, increasing holding costs. Common service level targets range from 90% to 99%, depending on the industry and product type.

Customer Expectations: Service level targets often depend on customer expectations. In industries with high competition, customers expect fast and reliable deliveries, necessitating higher service levels.

Product Importance: Companies may set different service levels for different products based on their importance or value. Critical items or items with high customer demand may have higher service levels, while less critical items may have lower service levels.

Analyzing Trade-offs:

Increasing service levels generally raises inventory holding costs due to higher safety stock requirements. Companies must evaluate the trade-off between improved service levels and increased costs to find the most efficient point.

Cost-Benefit Analysis: Cost-benefit analysis helps companies assess the financial impact of different service levels. For example, a 99% service level may provide excellent customer satisfaction but significantly increase costs, while a 95% service level could balance customer satisfaction with reasonable inventory costs.

Continuous Improvement and Monitoring:

Inventory policies should not remain static; they require regular evaluation and adjustment to account for changes in demand, costs, and market dynamics. By continuously monitoring inventory performance metrics, companies can identify opportunities to refine their policies.

Key Performance Indicators (KPIs): Monitoring KPIs like inventory turnover, stockout rates, and carrying costs provides insights into the effectiveness of current policies. For example, a high stockout rate might indicate the need for higher safety stock or better forecasting, while high carrying costs might suggest an opportunity to reduce safety stock.

Advanced Inventory Management Tools:

Technology plays a critical role in balancing service levels and costs. Inventory management software can automate reorder points, monitor stock levels in real time, and adjust safety stock dynamically based on demand fluctuations. These tools make it easier to maintain optimal inventory levels while keeping costs in check.

AI and Machine Learning: With advancements in AI and machine learning, companies can use predictive analytics to improve inventory policies. These tools analyze demand patterns and forecast trends, enabling more accurate reorder points and buffer stock levels.

In conclusion, setting inventory policies and targets is essential for achieving effective demand-driven inventory management. By selecting the right inventory review systems, establishing reorder points and safety stocks, and balancing service levels with costs, companies can optimize their inventory to meet customer demands efficiently. Leveraging technology and continuous improvement ensures that inventory policies remain aligned with the dynamic market conditions and changing customer expectations.

Chapter 7: Demand-Driven MRP (DDMRP) in Detail

As demand-driven inventory management continues to reshape modern supply chains, one methodology stands out for its ability to adapt to fluctuating demands and minimize stockouts—Demand-Driven MRP (DDMRP). This methodology refines traditional Material Requirements Planning (MRP) by adding demand-driven elements that align inventory levels with real-time demand patterns. In this chapter, we will delve into the core components of DDMRP, examine the benefits of this approach in dynamic environments, and explore real-world examples where companies have successfully implemented DDMRP to improve their supply chain performance.

Components of DDMRP: Strategic Inventory Positioning and Buffer Profiles

The DDMRP model includes several essential components designed to ensure that inventory is positioned correctly and optimized according to demand variability. Here, we break down two of the key elements: strategic inventory positioning and buffer profiles, which together form the backbone of a demand-driven approach.

Strategic Inventory Positioning:

Strategic inventory positioning is a core concept in DDMRP, which involves identifying key locations within the supply chain to hold inventory. These points, often referred to as "decoupling points," are strategically chosen to act as buffers, allowing the supply chain to absorb demand variability and avoid the bullwhip effect (a common issue where small fluctuations in demand lead to increasingly larger fluctuations upstream).

Decoupling Points: The purpose of decoupling points is to protect the flow of materials and goods from demand fluctuations. By strategically placing buffers at these points, companies can ensure that materials flow smoothly without stockouts or excess inventory.

Positioning Criteria: In DDMRP, positioning inventory is guided by factors like lead times, demand variability, and the criticality of certain materials. Decoupling points are typically chosen based on where inventory is most likely to experience significant delays or where demand variability is high. For example, a manufacturing company may position buffers at the point where raw materials enter production, or at stages with high variability in processing times.

Buffer Profiles and Levels:

Buffer profiles and levels are DDMRP's way of managing stock to meet demand while preventing overstocking. Buffers are set based on demand patterns, lead times, and other operational factors, and are divided into three zones: green, yellow, and red.

Red Zone: Represents the minimum stock level needed to protect against supply variability and ensure that production or delivery is not disrupted. This is the critical level of stock required to keep operations moving.

Yellow Zone: Acts as a middle ground, helping maintain an ideal inventory level to meet typical demand without excessive surplus. It reflects the anticipated demand based on recent trends.

Green Zone: The buffer's excess level, which acts as a reserve for spikes in demand or supply delays. Inventory in the green zone can be reduced or adjusted based on real-time demand data to avoid unnecessary holding costs.

Adjusting Buffer Profiles: Buffer profiles are dynamically adjusted based on changing demand patterns. For instance, in periods of high demand, DDMRP increases buffer levels, whereas in periods of low demand, it decreases them. This real-time adjustment prevents inventory buildup and reduces holding costs.

Color-Coded Management: The color-coded zones in DDMRP make it easy to visualize and manage inventory levels. Operators can see at a glance if an item is in the critical (red), alert (yellow), or excess (green) zone and take action accordingly.

Benefits of DDMRP for Dynamic Environments

DDMRP offers numerous advantages, especially in volatile, fast-paced markets where demand is constantly shifting. Here are several key benefits of implementing DDMRP:

Increased Responsiveness to Market Changes:

Traditional MRP systems work well in stable demand environments but often struggle to adapt quickly to market fluctuations. DDMRP, by contrast, is highly adaptive. It continuously monitors demand and adjusts buffers accordingly, allowing for quick responses to demand surges or drops. This agility helps businesses keep up with market changes without incurring high costs from overstocking or stockouts.

Reduction of the Bullwhip Effect:

The bullwhip effect, which occurs when small demand changes lead to larger fluctuations up the supply chain, is mitigated by DDMRP's strategic decoupling points. By positioning inventory at key stages in the supply chain, DDMRP absorbs variability, preventing these demand fluctuations from impacting suppliers and manufacturing schedules upstream.

Improved Inventory Efficiency:

DDMRP reduces the risk of carrying excess inventory by aligning stock levels with real-time demand. By setting dynamic buffer zones that respond to changes in demand and lead times, DDMRP enables companies to maintain leaner inventory levels without compromising service. This efficiency translates into lower carrying costs and less capital tied up in stock, which can be reinvested in other areas of the business.

Enhanced Customer Satisfaction and Service Levels:

By keeping critical inventory positioned and readily available at decoupling points, DDMRP ensures that stockouts are minimized and customer orders are fulfilled on time. This improved service level increases customer satisfaction and enhances the company's reputation for reliability.

Simplified Inventory Management:

The color-coded buffer zones (red, yellow, green) make inventory levels easy to monitor and manage. Operators can quickly assess inventory status and take corrective action if any item is at risk of running low or accumulating too much stock. This simplicity makes DDMRP accessible and easy to implement, even in complex environments.

Alignment with Lean and Agile Principles:

DDMRP's focus on pull-based replenishment aligns with lean principles, which seek to minimize waste and optimize flow within the supply chain. Similarly, the flexibility and responsiveness of DDMRP resonate with agile practices, helping companies respond swiftly to changes in demand without overcommitting resources.

Case Studies of Successful DDMRP Implementation

Many companies across industries have adopted DDMRP to optimize their supply chains and achieve greater resilience. Here are a few examples that illustrate how DDMRP can deliver substantial benefits in real-world settings.

General Electric (GE):

GE implemented DDMRP in their aviation and power divisions to better manage the complex, high-stakes inventory that supports their global manufacturing operations. Prior to DDMRP, GE's inventory was managed with traditional MRP, leading to issues with overstocking in some regions and stockouts in others.

Results: With DDMRP, GE was able to strategically position inventory buffers at critical points in their supply chain, resulting in a 20% reduction in lead times and a 30% improvement in on-time delivery rates. The company also saw an overall reduction in inventory carrying costs as buffer stock levels were optimized to align with demand.

Siemens:

Siemens applied DDMRP to their industrial automation division, where high product variability and fluctuating customer demand presented significant challenges. By shifting to a demand-driven approach, Siemens was able to reduce the complexity of their inventory management processes.

Results: Siemens reported a 25% improvement in inventory turnover and a 15% reduction in overall inventory levels within the first year of implementation. The company was also able to improve service levels by ensuring that critical components were readily available when needed, even during peak demand periods.

Unilever:

Unilever implemented DDMRP in their supply chain for consumer goods to address demand variability across multiple geographic markets. Traditional MRP methods had led to excess inventory in some locations, while other areas struggled with stockouts due to unforeseen demand spikes.

Results: With DDMRP, Unilever was able to reduce stockouts by 40% and achieve higher fill rates, improving customer satisfaction significantly. Additionally, Unilever benefited from a 10% reduction in inventory holding costs by strategically positioning inventory buffers and reducing waste.

Volkswagen:

Volkswagen adopted DDMRP in its parts and accessories distribution centers, where unpredictable customer demand for spare parts made it difficult to maintain optimal inventory levels. By implementing DDMRP, Volkswagen created buffer profiles to account for different parts' demand patterns and supply lead times.

Results: Volkswagen's switch to DDMRP led to a 15% improvement in service level and a 12% reduction in inventory costs. The demand-driven approach also helped Volkswagen manage the complexities of a global supply chain and reduce the impact of demand variability on their distribution operations.

DDMRP is a powerful tool for companies operating in dynamic and competitive environments. By aligning inventory with actual demand patterns, DDMRP enables businesses to optimize their stock levels, improve service rates, and reduce costs associated with excess inventory. The methodology's core components—strategic inventory positioning, buffer profiles, and dynamic adjustments—give companies the flexibility and responsiveness needed to navigate today's volatile supply chains. Through case studies, we can see the tangible impact DDMRP has made on businesses across various industries, demonstrating its effectiveness in enhancing supply chain performance and customer satisfaction.

Chapter 8: Demand Sensing and Demand Shaping

The rapid pace of today's markets requires businesses to stay closely aligned with customer demand to maintain a competitive edge. This chapter delves into two critical strategies for aligning inventory management with market demand: demand sensing and demand shaping. Together, these strategies enable companies to more accurately anticipate, respond to, and influence customer demand, allowing for improved service levels, optimized inventory levels, and reduced costs. Here, we explore the role of real-time data in demand sensing, discuss techniques for shaping demand, and examine how these approaches can be effectively integrated into inventory management.

Introduction to Demand Sensing: Using Real-Time Data

Traditional forecasting methods often rely on historical data and generalized assumptions, which may not account for sudden shifts in customer demand, seasonal trends, or external events. Demand sensing offers a solution by providing near real-time insights into demand patterns. Using advanced data analytics and machine learning, demand sensing can capture and interpret real-time data from a variety of sources, including point-of-sale systems, customer transactions, social media, and even weather forecasts.

Definition of Demand Sensing:

Demand sensing is the process of using current, real-time data to adjust short-term forecasts and improve responsiveness to demand changes. Unlike traditional forecasting, which is often limited by historical data, demand sensing leverages predictive analytics to provide immediate insights and enable more responsive decision-making.

Data Sources for Demand Sensing:

Demand sensing draws from multiple data sources to create a comprehensive view of current market demand. Key sources include:

Point-of-Sale (POS) Data: Retailers collect POS data at checkout, providing insights into customer buying behavior and preferences in real time.

E-commerce Data: Online sales data, such as clicks, search patterns, and cart abandonment rates, reveal customer interest and demand trends.

Social Media Trends: Social listening tools track brand mentions, trends, and customer sentiment, giving an early indication of demand shifts.

Weather and Event Data: In industries like fashion, food, and beverage, demand is often influenced by weather patterns and major events. Integrating this data helps companies prepare for anticipated demand changes.

Technology for Demand Sensing:

Demand sensing relies on machine learning and artificial intelligence (AI) to process and analyze large data sets. Advanced algorithms can detect patterns, spot anomalies, and even predict demand shifts, allowing businesses to adjust inventory levels dynamically.

Predictive Analytics: By analyzing historical trends alongside real-time data, predictive analytics helps identify future demand spikes or lulls, enabling proactive inventory adjustments.

Machine Learning Models: Machine learning models continuously learn from new data and refine their predictions, allowing them to detect trends that traditional statistical models may miss.

Benefits of Demand Sensing in Inventory Management:

Enhanced Responsiveness: Demand sensing enables companies to react quickly to changing market conditions, reducing the likelihood of stockouts or overstock.

Inventory Optimization: Real-time insights allow for fine-tuning of stock levels, reducing excess inventory and associated holding costs.

Improved Forecast Accuracy: By supplementing traditional forecasts with real-time data, demand sensing enhances forecast accuracy, leading to better alignment between supply and demand.

Demand Shaping Techniques: Promotions, Pricing, and Product Positioning

While demand sensing is about responding to existing demand, demand shaping is about actively influencing it. Demand shaping involves strategies that alter consumer behavior to smoothen or increase demand, reducing volatility and ensuring a more balanced approach to inventory management.

Definition of Demand Shaping:

Demand shaping refers to techniques that actively encourage customer purchases through strategies such as promotions, pricing adjustments, and product placement. The goal is to align demand with business objectives and prevent imbalances that may lead to excess inventory or shortages.

Key Demand Shaping Techniques:

There are various ways businesses can shape demand, including:

Promotions and Discounts: Offering temporary discounts or promotions can boost sales during low-demand periods, helping to reduce excess inventory.

Dynamic Pricing: Adjusting prices based on demand levels can help manage inventory flow. For instance, higher prices may be applied during peak demand to manage stock levels, while discounts can stimulate demand when sales are slow.

Product Positioning: Strategically positioning products in high-visibility areas, whether online or in-store, increases exposure and can drive higher sales.

Product Bundling: Grouping complementary products together encourages additional purchases and can be effective for moving slower-selling items alongside popular ones.

Advantages of Demand Shaping:

Demand shaping allows companies to better manage inventory and reduce waste by smoothing demand patterns, making it easier to anticipate and fulfill customer needs.

Reduced Stockouts: By actively shaping demand, businesses can prevent stockouts during high-demand periods, ensuring customers always have access to desired products.

Enhanced Profit Margins: Strategic demand shaping, especially through pricing strategies, can enhance profitability by maximizing revenue during peak demand periods.

Challenges in Demand Shaping:

Customer Perception: Frequent price changes or promotions may lead to price-sensitive customers who only buy during sales, which can reduce profitability in the long run.

Operational Complexity: Demand shaping strategies often require careful coordination between sales, marketing, and inventory management, and may increase complexity.

Integrating Demand Sensing and Shaping into Inventory Management

For businesses to reap the full benefits of demand-driven inventory management, it's essential to integrate both demand sensing and demand shaping strategies within their broader inventory management processes. By combining real-time insights with proactive demand manipulation, companies can achieve a holistic approach to aligning inventory with actual market needs.

Creating a Feedback Loop Between Sensing and Shaping:

Demand sensing and shaping should not function in isolation but as part of a continuous feedback loop. For example, data from demand sensing can reveal which products are currently trending, allowing the business to focus its demand shaping efforts (such as promotions) on those products.

Real-Time Adjustments: As demand sensing data highlights fluctuations, companies can immediately employ demand shaping strategies—such as targeted promotions—to address any potential surges or drops, ensuring optimal stock levels.

Technology and Systems Integration:

To fully integrate demand sensing and shaping, companies require sophisticated technology platforms that can gather, analyze, and act on real-time data. Many companies use advanced ERP and inventory management systems to combine demand sensing and shaping capabilities, allowing them to respond dynamically to market conditions.

Artificial Intelligence (AI) and Machine Learning: AI-powered systems can automate much of the demand sensing and shaping process. For instance, machine learning algorithms can trigger price changes or promotions based on real-time demand insights without manual intervention.

Developing Cross-Functional Teams:

Integrating demand sensing and shaping requires collaboration across multiple departments, including sales, marketing, supply chain, and inventory management. Cross-functional teams can ensure that all parts of the organization work together to align inventory levels with demand.

Alignment of Goals: These teams must have a shared understanding of the company's inventory and sales goals to ensure that demand sensing and shaping strategies align with broader business objectives.

Case Study: Demand Sensing and Shaping in Action:

Example – A Global Consumer Goods Company:

A large consumer goods company implemented demand sensing to monitor sales trends across its extensive network of retail partners. The company used data from POS systems and social media to detect shifts in demand, which it fed into its demand shaping strategies. When sensing data indicated a spike in demand for certain products, the company launched targeted promotions and adjusted pricing to capture additional sales and prevent stockouts.

Results: The company experienced a 15% increase in forecast accuracy and a 20% reduction in stockouts, while also improving customer satisfaction. By shaping demand in response to real-time insights, the company was able to maintain optimal inventory levels and boost profitability.

Demand sensing and shaping provide powerful tools for businesses seeking to optimize their inventory management in an increasingly volatile market. By leveraging real-time data to adjust forecasts and employing demand-shaping tactics to influence consumer behavior, companies can achieve a demand-driven approach that is both responsive and proactive. Together, these strategies empower companies to enhance service levels, reduce waste, and maintain inventory levels that align closely with actual market demand. As we continue in this demand-driven journey, the integration of these capabilities becomes critical for businesses looking to stay competitive and responsive to the dynamic needs of the market.

Chapter 9: Sales and Operations Planning (S&OP)

Sales and Operations Planning (S&OP) is a vital process for demand-driven inventory management, bridging the gap between different business functions to align supply, demand, and inventory levels. This chapter explores the critical role of S&OP in creating a unified, demand-responsive approach to inventory management, enhancing both operational efficiency and strategic alignment. By balancing supply and demand, S&OP enables companies to optimize inventory levels, reduce costs, and meet customer expectations, all while aligning inventory strategies with broader company goals.

The Role of S&OP in Demand-Driven Inventory Management

In a demand-driven inventory management environment, S&OP serves as the cornerstone of alignment across the business. It brings together various functions—such as sales, operations, finance, and supply chain—through a structured, collaborative process that drives unified decision-making and planning. The primary goal of S&OP is to ensure that a company's inventory strategies are responsive to real customer demand, allowing for an agile and adaptive approach to inventory management.

What is S&OP?

Sales and Operations Planning is a structured process that facilitates cross-functional collaboration to create a balanced plan for demand and supply. Typically, S&OP involves regular monthly or quarterly meetings where teams review forecasts, assess inventory needs, align resources, and make necessary adjustments.

By ensuring that all functions work toward shared goals, S&OP aligns supply chain activities with overall business objectives, creating a more demand-responsive approach to inventory management.

Core Objectives of S&OP in Demand-Driven Environments:

Improve Forecast Accuracy: By involving multiple stakeholders, S&OP can produce more accurate and reliable demand forecasts, allowing for better planning and inventory positioning.

Enhance Agility: Through regular reviews and updates, S&OP enables companies to respond swiftly to market changes, ensuring that inventory remains aligned with demand.

Reduce Costs: By balancing inventory levels with real demand, S&OP reduces holding costs, minimizes stockouts, and ensures that resources are allocated efficiently.

How S&OP Differs in Demand-Driven Models:

Unlike traditional, production-centered inventory management, a demand-driven S&OP approach focuses on customer needs as the starting point for planning. Demand signals and real-time data are continuously integrated, creating a flexible approach that prioritizes customer responsiveness over production efficiency alone.

Key Elements of a Demand-Driven S&OP Process:

Cross-Functional Collaboration: S&OP requires close collaboration across departments, breaking down silos to ensure a unified approach to managing inventory in response to demand changes.

Demand-Supply Balancing: The process seeks to create a balance between available supply and anticipated demand, minimizing both overstock and shortages.

Regular Review and Adjustment: Demand-driven S&OP involves ongoing evaluation, with monthly or quarterly meetings to ensure that plans remain aligned with real-time market conditions.

Balancing Supply and Demand Effectively

An effective S&OP process centers on balancing supply with actual demand, aiming to maintain optimal inventory levels and prevent costly mismatches between what customers need and what's available in stock. Demand-driven S&OP enhances this balance by incorporating real-time demand data, improving both short-term flexibility and long-term strategic alignment.

Supply-Demand Alignment as a Core S&OP Function:

Demand-driven S&OP ensures that customer needs guide supply chain activities. By continuously balancing supply and demand, S&OP helps prevent the inefficiencies that come from relying solely on historical forecasts.

This alignment reduces the risk of stockouts during demand peaks and avoids excessive inventory buildup during periods of low demand.

Steps in Balancing Supply and Demand:

Forecasting: The starting point is an accurate demand forecast, informed by historical data, current market trends, and input from sales and marketing.

Supply Planning: Once demand is forecasted, supply chain teams work to develop a corresponding plan to meet that demand, adjusting production schedules and inventory policies as needed.

Gap Analysis and Reconciliation: S&OP meetings often include a review of gaps between supply and demand. Teams discuss how best to reconcile these gaps through adjustments to inventory, production, or procurement.

Action Plan and Monitoring: Based on the reconciliation, teams create action plans and continuously monitor progress, making adjustments as real-time demand data evolves.

Demand Shaping within S&OP:

In demand-driven S&OP, demand shaping strategies such as promotions or dynamic pricing are often used to balance supply and demand. This can be particularly useful during anticipated demand fluctuations or supply constraints, where influencing customer purchasing behavior can smooth demand patterns and maintain balanced inventory levels.

The Role of Technology in Balancing Supply and Demand:

S&OP processes benefit significantly from technology platforms that provide real-time visibility into supply, demand, and inventory levels. Advanced S&OP software and ERP systems facilitate integrated data analysis, enabling teams to make quicker, data-driven adjustments.

Aligning Inventory Strategies with Company Goals

Demand-driven S&OP doesn't just optimize operational efficiency; it also ensures that inventory management aligns with the broader goals and strategy of the organization. This alignment creates a cohesive approach where inventory decisions contribute directly to business objectives, whether they're focused on growth, cost reduction, or enhanced customer satisfaction.

Connecting Inventory Management with Business Strategy:

S&OP provides a structured process for aligning inventory strategies with high-level company goals. For instance, if the company's strategic focus is on rapid market responsiveness, S&OP can help position inventory to prioritize availability in key markets.

Similarly, for companies with a strong focus on cost control, S&OP can focus on strategies that minimize inventory holding costs, such as lean inventory policies and just-in-time replenishment.

Setting S&OP Goals Aligned with Company Objectives:

Service Level Targets: Establishing service level targets within S&OP helps align inventory policies with customer satisfaction goals. Higher service levels may require more buffer stock, while a lower service level target may focus more on cost savings.

Cost Objectives: Inventory strategies can also be aligned to achieve cost-related goals. For example, S&OP can drive decisions to reduce carrying costs by optimizing reorder points and leveraging economies of scale.

Growth and Market Expansion: For companies focused on growth, S&OP can play a role in managing inventory levels across multiple locations, supporting rapid market expansion without sacrificing product availability.

Key Performance Indicators (KPIs) for S&OP Success:

S&OP success is often measured through KPIs that reflect both operational efficiency and alignment with business objectives. Common S&OP KPIs include forecast accuracy, inventory turnover, stockouts, and service levels.

Customer-Focused KPIs: Metrics like on-time delivery rates and customer satisfaction scores provide insight into how well the S&OP process supports customer needs.

Cost and Efficiency KPIs: Inventory carrying cost, days of supply, and order fulfillment lead time help evaluate the cost-effectiveness of the inventory strategy within the S&OP framework.

Case Study: Successful Alignment of S&OP with Company Goals:

Example – A Global Electronics Manufacturer:

The company implemented an S&OP process to align its inventory strategy with its objective of rapid market responsiveness. By integrating real-time demand data and fostering cross-functional collaboration, the company was able to reduce stockouts and improve its inventory turnover rate by 25%.

Outcome: The S&OP process not only optimized inventory levels but also enhanced customer satisfaction and supported the company's strategic goal of becoming the fastest provider in its market segment.

71

Sales and Operations Planning (S&OP) provides a powerful framework for aligning inventory management with customer demand and organizational objectives in a demand-driven context. By balancing supply and demand, facilitating cross-functional collaboration, and aligning inventory strategies with broader company goals, S&OP becomes a strategic tool that enhances both operational efficiency and market responsiveness. As companies continue to adopt demand-driven practices, S&OP remains a foundational process for ensuring that inventory levels, supply chain activities, and business objectives work in harmony, ultimately supporting sustainable growth and long-term success.

Chapter 10: Inventory Optimization Techniques

Inventory optimization is a crucial component of demand-driven inventory management, ensuring that businesses maintain the right levels of stock at the right time and in the right locations. Effective inventory optimization not only minimizes costs but also enhances service levels, enabling organizations to meet customer demand while reducing excess inventory. This chapter explores various inventory optimization techniques, including key optimization models such as Economic Order Quantity (EOQ) and ABC analysis, multi-echelon inventory optimization, and the tools and software that assist in inventory optimization.

Optimization Models: Economic Order Quantity (EOQ), ABC Analysis

1. Economic Order Quantity (EOQ)

The Economic Order Quantity (EOQ) is one of the oldest and most widely used inventory optimization models. It provides a formula for determining the optimal order quantity that minimizes total inventory costs, including both ordering and holding costs. The EOQ model assumes that demand, ordering costs, and holding costs are constant over time.

Key Elements of EOQ:

Demand Rate (D): The number of units needed per time period.

Ordering Cost (S): The fixed cost incurred each time an order is placed, regardless of order size (e.g., transportation, administrative costs).

Holding Cost (H): The cost of holding one unit in inventory for a specified period (e.g., storage costs, insurance, depreciation).

The EOQ formula is expressed as:

$$EOQ = \sqrt{\frac{2DS}{H}}$$

Where:

D = demand rate

S = ordering cost

H = holding cost

Benefits of EOQ:

It minimizes the total cost by determining the most cost-effective order quantity.

EOQ helps in balancing ordering and holding costs by identifying an optimal order size that reduces waste and inefficiencies.

EOQ is particularly useful for companies with steady demand and relatively predictable costs.

Limitations of EOQ:

EOQ assumes constant demand and order costs, which may not always hold true in real-world scenarios.

It is less effective in dynamic environments where demand fluctuates significantly or where lead times are uncertain.

2. ABC Analysis

ABC analysis is an inventory management technique that classifies inventory items based on their value to the organization. It categorizes items into three groups—A, B, and C—depending on their importance and the impact they have on overall inventory costs. This technique is particularly useful for prioritizing inventory management efforts and optimizing inventory levels.

Classification:

A Items: These are high-value items that contribute the most to the overall inventory value but may not be the largest in quantity. These items require careful inventory control and frequent monitoring.

B Items: These are mid-range items in terms of value and volume. They are less critical than A items but still require periodic reviews and more moderate control.

C Items: These are low-value items that make up the largest portion of the inventory in terms of volume but contribute little to total inventory value. These items require minimal attention and are managed with simple reorder systems.

Benefits of ABC Analysis:

Helps businesses focus resources on the most important inventory items.

Allows companies to optimize stock levels based on item importance, reducing the cost of carrying unnecessary inventory.

Enables more efficient stock replenishment processes for A items and streamlined management of B and C items.

Challenges of ABC Analysis:

It assumes that value can be measured solely by cost, but other factors like lead time or criticality to operations may also play a role.

The classification may change over time, requiring regular reviews and adjustments.

Multi-Echelon Inventory Optimization

Multi-echelon inventory optimization involves optimizing inventory across multiple stages or locations in a supply chain, from suppliers to warehouses to retail stores. Unlike traditional inventory management, which focuses on individual stock levels at a single location, multi-echelon optimization aims to improve overall supply chain efficiency by considering the interactions between various levels of inventory.

Key Concepts in Multi-Echelon Optimization:

Multiple Inventory Locations: A multi-echelon system considers inventory across several locations, such as manufacturing plants, distribution centers, and retail outlets. Each location must maintain inventory levels that both satisfy local demand and contribute to the overall system's efficiency.

Interdependencies Between Echelons: Inventory at one echelon impacts the inventory needs of the next echelon. For example, a shortage at a warehouse will lead to stockouts at retail locations, while excess inventory at a warehouse can lead to unnecessary holding costs.

Demand Propagation: Demand at the consumer level can propagate upstream, requiring coordination across the entire supply chain to ensure that inventory is positioned correctly at each echelon.

Optimization Models for Multi-Echelon Systems:

Network Optimization Models: These models account for the entire supply chain network, factoring in transportation, lead times, and distribution costs to determine the most efficient inventory levels across all locations.

Safety Stock Calculations: In multi-echelon systems, safety stock levels need to be optimized at each echelon to account for demand variability, lead time uncertainty, and stockouts at downstream locations.

Total Cost Minimization: The goal of multi-echelon optimization is to minimize total costs across the entire supply chain, balancing holding costs, ordering costs, transportation costs, and the risk of stockouts.

Benefits of Multi-Echelon Inventory Optimization:

It reduces the total cost of inventory across the supply chain by optimizing stock levels at each echelon.

Improves service levels by ensuring that inventory is available where and when it is needed.

Increases flexibility in responding to changes in demand or supply chain disruptions.

Challenges in Multi-Echelon Optimization:

Complex to model and implement, particularly in large supply chains with many echelons.

Requires real-time data and sophisticated software tools to track inventory across multiple locations and make timely adjustments.

It can be resource-intensive, requiring continuous monitoring and adjustments to keep inventory levels in sync.

Tools and Software for Inventory Optimization

In today's dynamic supply chain environment, businesses rely on sophisticated software tools and technologies to optimize inventory. These tools leverage advanced algorithms, real-time data, and predictive analytics to provide recommendations and insights that improve inventory management and reduce costs. Below are some of the key tools and software solutions used for inventory optimization.

1. Enterprise Resource Planning (ERP) Systems

ERP systems, such as SAP, Oracle, and Microsoft Dynamics, integrate various business functions, including finance, procurement, production, and sales. Many modern ERP systems feature modules for inventory management that enable businesses to optimize stock levels, track inventory in real-time, and align inventory with demand.

Benefits:

Provide a unified view of inventory data across multiple locations.

Automate reorder processes and help set safety stock levels based on demand forecasts.

Integrate with other business systems for enhanced decision-making.

2. Inventory Management Software

Specialized inventory management software, such as NetSuite, TradeGecko, and Fishbowl, is designed to handle the complexities of inventory optimization, particularly for small and medium-sized businesses. These tools offer features such as demand forecasting, stock tracking, and order management, making them ideal for businesses looking to streamline their inventory processes.

Benefits:

Real-time inventory tracking and automatic updates.

Easy integration with other business functions like sales and procurement.

Reporting and analytics to help optimize reorder points and stock levels.

3. Advanced Analytics and Optimization Tools

Advanced tools like Llamasoft, Kinaxis, and JDA (now Blue Yonder) offer sophisticated inventory optimization algorithms that consider multiple factors, such as demand variability, lead time, transportation costs, and supply chain constraints. These platforms provide end-to-end optimization capabilities for both single-location and multi-echelon systems.

Benefits:

Provide predictive analytics to anticipate demand fluctuations and adjust inventory levels accordingly.

Use machine learning to optimize inventory replenishment decisions.

Offer real-time decision support to enhance supply chain responsiveness.

4. Demand Forecasting Software

Demand forecasting software, such as Forecast Pro, Demand Solutions, and Oracle Demantra, helps companies improve the accuracy of their demand forecasts, which is a critical component of inventory optimization. By using historical data, market trends, and machine learning, these tools provide more accurate demand predictions, which in turn allows businesses to optimize inventory levels.

Benefits:

Improved forecast accuracy through advanced statistical models.

Integration with other inventory management systems for seamless data sharing.

Real-time forecasting capabilities to support rapid decision-making.

Inventory optimization is a dynamic and ongoing process that requires a combination of the right models, techniques, and tools. By utilizing models like EOQ and ABC analysis, businesses can optimize their order quantities and prioritize inventory management efforts. Multi-echelon inventory optimization takes this a step further by considering the entire supply chain network, ensuring inventory is positioned effectively across multiple locations. Modern inventory management tools, powered by advanced analytics, demand sensing, and real-time data, enable businesses to implement these techniques efficiently, helping them reduce costs, enhance service levels, and maintain responsiveness in an increasingly complex and competitive marketplace.

Chapter 11: Lead Time Management

Lead time is one of the most critical elements in demand-driven inventory management. It directly affects the amount of inventory a company must hold to meet customer demand without experiencing stockouts or excess inventory. Properly managing lead time helps businesses optimize their inventory levels, reduce holding costs, and improve service levels. In this chapter, we will explore how lead time impacts inventory needs, how companies can reduce lead times through process improvements, and the effect of lead time variability on demand-driven inventory systems.

How Lead Time Impacts Inventory Needs

Lead time is defined as the time it takes for a product to move from order placement to delivery. This includes several components, such as procurement lead time (for raw materials), production lead time (for manufacturing), transportation lead time (for delivery from suppliers or distribution centers), and any delays within the process. Understanding lead time is crucial for determining the right amount of inventory to maintain and when to reorder stock.

Key Impacts of Lead Time on Inventory Management:

Reorder Points: The reorder point (ROP) is the inventory level at which a new order should be placed to avoid stockouts. Lead time plays a critical role in determining the ROP, as longer lead times require higher levels of safety stock to prevent running out of inventory during the replenishment period. The basic formula for ROP is:

ROP=(AverageDemandperPeriod×LeadTime)+SafetyStock

As lead time increases, the safety stock must also increase to accommodate for the uncertainty in delivery time, thus increasing overall inventory requirements.

Stockouts and Service Levels: Longer lead times increase the risk of stockouts. A delay in the replenishment process can cause stockouts, affecting service levels and customer satisfaction. On the other hand, holding too much inventory to cover longer lead times increases holding costs and ties up capital in unsold goods. This trade-off between stockouts and holding costs makes it essential to carefully manage lead time.

Inventory Turnover: Companies with long lead times often experience slower inventory turnover because they must hold larger quantities of stock to accommodate the lead time. This reduces efficiency in the supply chain and ties up valuable resources that could be used elsewhere in the business.

Buffer Stock Levels: To mitigate the risk of stockouts due to long lead times, businesses often keep buffer stock (extra inventory) on hand. However, increasing buffer stock to account for longer lead times also increases the costs associated with holding excess inventory. Therefore, balancing inventory levels with lead time is a critical factor in reducing overall supply chain costs.

Reducing Lead Times Through Process Improvements

Reducing lead time is one of the most effective ways to optimize inventory management. By shortening lead times, companies can reduce the amount of inventory they need to hold, lower costs, and improve their responsiveness to demand fluctuations. Several process improvements can help reduce lead times:

1. Supplier Relationship Management and Collaboration

Strategic Supplier Partnerships: Building strong, collaborative relationships with suppliers can significantly reduce procurement lead times. By working closely with key suppliers, businesses can ensure faster processing of orders, reduce the time needed for sourcing materials, and ensure a more predictable supply chain.

Supplier Performance Metrics: Monitoring and setting expectations for suppliers can help reduce lead time. Key performance indicators (KPIs) such as on-time delivery rates, quality control standards, and lead time consistency can help businesses identify and address performance issues that contribute to delays.

Vendor-Managed Inventory (VMI): With VMI, suppliers monitor inventory levels at the customer's location and are responsible for replenishing stock when it reaches a predefined level. This reduces procurement lead times and ensures that stock is always available without requiring the customer to place orders manually.

2. Lean Manufacturing and Process Streamlining

Reducing Internal Process Delays: Inefficiencies in the manufacturing or assembly process can significantly contribute to lead time. By implementing lean principles, such as eliminating bottlenecks, reducing waste, and streamlining production workflows, companies can reduce production lead times. Techniques such as value stream mapping can help identify and eliminate unnecessary steps in the process, improving overall flow and reducing delays.

Just-in-Time (JIT) Production: JIT is a production strategy that focuses on producing goods only when they are needed. This minimizes waiting times and reduces inventory levels. By aligning production schedules closely with customer demand, JIT helps reduce the lead time required for production and minimizes stockpiling of raw materials.

Cross-Functional Collaboration: Improved coordination between departments, such as procurement, manufacturing, and distribution, can streamline processes and reduce delays. Cross-functional teams can address issues early in the process and implement improvements that reduce lead time.

3. Automation and Technology Integration

Automating Ordering Systems: Automating procurement and ordering systems helps speed up the replenishment process by reducing manual errors, increasing order accuracy, and speeding up the response time between placing orders and receiving products.

Advanced Planning and Scheduling (APS) Systems: APS systems use real-time data to plan and schedule production and procurement activities. By integrating data from across the supply chain, businesses can optimize schedules, reduce production delays, and shorten lead times. These systems can also provide more accurate forecasts and demand-driven scheduling, ensuring that production is aligned with actual demand.

Robotics and AI in Manufacturing: Using robotics and artificial intelligence (AI) in manufacturing processes can further reduce production lead times by automating repetitive tasks, improving precision, and speeding up the production cycle.

Lead Time Variability and Its Effect on Demand-Driven Inventory

While lead time reduction is a key goal for improving inventory management, lead time variability—fluctuations or uncertainty in the time it takes to receive goods—poses significant challenges. Variability in lead times can have a profound impact on inventory levels and the ability to meet customer demand.

Challenges Posed by Lead Time Variability:

Increased Safety Stock Requirements: When lead time is variable, companies must increase safety stock to buffer against the uncertainty. This can lead to higher inventory holding costs. The more unpredictable the lead time, the larger the safety stock buffer needed to ensure that the business does not run out of stock during periods of longer lead times.

Demand Fluctuations: Lead time variability can also exacerbate issues with demand variability. If lead time fluctuates, it becomes difficult to accurately predict when stock will be replenished, making it harder to align inventory levels with actual customer demand. This can lead to either stockouts or overstocking, both of which are costly.

Order Cycle Misalignment: Variability in lead time can also cause misalignment between inventory levels and actual demand cycles. If the replenishment process is delayed, there may be a lag in satisfying customer demand, while an unexpectedly quick replenishment cycle may cause excess stock, leading to inefficiency.

Managing Lead Time Variability:

Buffering Against Variability: One of the primary ways to manage lead time variability is to increase safety stock. However, this comes with the trade-off of higher holding costs. The key is to find the optimal buffer size that can handle most variations in lead time without excessive inventory buildup.

Supplier Diversity: Relying on multiple suppliers for critical components or products can help reduce lead time variability. By diversifying suppliers, businesses can mitigate the risk of long lead times from a single supplier, ensuring that inventory replenishment is less affected by disruptions in the supply chain.

Lead Time Monitoring and Communication: Implementing systems to track lead time in real-time is essential for managing variability. By closely monitoring lead time performance, businesses can identify patterns and adjust their ordering strategies accordingly. Real-time tracking also helps improve communication with suppliers, making it easier to anticipate delays and adjust inventory levels proactively.

Lead time management is a critical component of demand-driven inventory systems. By understanding the impact of lead time on inventory needs and implementing strategies to reduce lead times, businesses can improve efficiency, reduce holding costs, and enhance customer service. Moreover, managing lead time variability is essential for maintaining inventory levels that are closely aligned with actual demand while avoiding stockouts and excessive stock buildup. Process improvements, technology integration, and strategic supplier relationships all contribute to lead time reduction, making it possible for businesses to better respond to changes in demand and reduce their reliance on buffer stock. Effective lead time management is a cornerstone of a lean, demand-driven inventory system, helping businesses remain competitive in an increasingly fast-paced and dynamic marketplace.

Chapter 12: Supplier Collaboration and Its Impact on Inventory

In demand-driven inventory management, supplier collaboration is essential for streamlining the supply chain, improving lead times, and reducing inventory costs. By working closely with suppliers, companies can reduce uncertainties in the replenishment process, enhance inventory visibility, and align inventory management strategies with actual demand. This chapter delves into the importance of building strong supplier relationships, explores vendor-managed inventory (VMI) and collaborative planning practices, and examines how supplier performance and reliability influence inventory management success.

Building Strong Supplier Relationships to Reduce Lead Times

Collaborative relationships with suppliers are a foundation for effective inventory management. When companies foster trust and transparency with their suppliers, they gain access to better information, faster response times, and higher service levels. Strong supplier relationships directly impact lead times, allowing companies to minimize delays and maintain optimal inventory levels.

1. Transparency and Open Communication:

Transparent communication enables companies and suppliers to align on objectives, share demand forecasts, and adjust order quantities and schedules as needed. When suppliers are informed about demand fluctuations, they can prepare their resources accordingly, which can reduce lead times and improve service levels.

Regular communication also promotes early detection of potential issues in the supply chain, allowing companies and suppliers to collaboratively address any bottlenecks or delays before they impact inventory.

2. Joint Problem-Solving and Continuous Improvement:

Companies that maintain collaborative relationships with suppliers can work together to resolve issues that affect lead times, such as production inefficiencies, quality concerns, or logistical bottlenecks. By jointly identifying root causes and implementing solutions, they can minimize the impact of these issues on inventory and enhance supply chain resilience.

Collaborative improvement efforts can also lead to innovations in production and delivery, potentially reducing lead times and improving the efficiency of the replenishment process.

3. Flexibility and Adaptability:

Supplier flexibility is crucial in demand-driven inventory systems. Building strong relationships enables companies to negotiate more flexible order terms and conditions, such as quicker order fulfillment, shorter lead times, or the ability to adjust orders in response to sudden changes in demand.

Flexible suppliers are more likely to accommodate last-minute adjustments or rush orders, which helps businesses avoid stockouts and maintain service levels in volatile demand environments.

Vendor-Managed Inventory (VMI) and Collaborative Planning

Vendor-managed inventory (VMI) and collaborative planning are two powerful practices that enable closer collaboration between suppliers and companies. Through these practices, suppliers take on a more active role in managing inventory, while companies benefit from reduced stockouts, lower holding costs, and more efficient inventory management.

1. Vendor-Managed Inventory (VMI):

Overview: In a VMI arrangement, the supplier is responsible for monitoring and managing the customer's inventory levels. The supplier regularly replenishes inventory based on agreed-upon targets, eliminating the need for the customer to place orders manually. This arrangement streamlines the ordering process, reduces lead times, and improves inventory availability.

Benefits of VMI:

Reduced Stockouts and Improved Service Levels: Since the supplier has real-time visibility into inventory levels, they can proactively replenish stock, reducing the risk of stockouts and ensuring that inventory is available to meet demand.

Lower Inventory Holding Costs: With VMI, companies can maintain lower safety stock levels since suppliers are responsible for ensuring that inventory is replenished as needed. This helps reduce carrying costs and improves overall cost efficiency.

Enhanced Forecast Accuracy: Suppliers participating in VMI often have access to more accurate and up-to-date demand data, which enables them to make more informed replenishment decisions and minimize overstocking.

2. Collaborative Planning, Forecasting, and Replenishment (CPFR):

Overview: CPFR is a structured approach to supplier collaboration that involves jointly developing forecasts, planning for demand, and coordinating replenishment schedules. CPFR is based on the premise that companies and suppliers can achieve better results by working together to align their planning processes.

93

Benefits of CPFR:

Improved Forecast Accuracy: By sharing demand forecasts, sales data, and inventory information, both parties gain insights into market trends and demand fluctuations, leading to more accurate and aligned forecasts.

Reduced Lead Times and Order Cycle Times: With a clear understanding of demand expectations, suppliers can plan their production schedules more efficiently, which reduces lead times and shortens the time between order placement and delivery.

Better Demand Responsiveness: CPFR allows companies and suppliers to coordinate replenishment efforts more effectively, making it easier to respond to unexpected spikes or drops in demand and ensuring that inventory levels align with actual customer needs.

Supplier Performance and Reliability

The success of demand-driven inventory management depends heavily on supplier performance and reliability. Reliable suppliers enable companies to maintain leaner inventory levels and avoid the need for excessive safety stock. Conversely, inconsistent supplier performance can lead to frequent stockouts, excess inventory, and increased costs.

1. Assessing Supplier Performance:

Key Performance Indicators (KPIs): Tracking KPIs such as on-time delivery, order accuracy, quality of goods, and responsiveness to changes is essential for assessing supplier performance. These metrics provide a clear picture of how well suppliers meet expectations and fulfill their commitments.

Supplier Scorecards: Supplier scorecards are a valuable tool for evaluating supplier performance over time. By using scorecards, companies can rate suppliers on various performance criteria, identify areas for improvement, and make informed decisions about which suppliers to work with closely.

Risk Assessment: Evaluating suppliers' risk profiles is also crucial, as high-risk suppliers (e.g., those in volatile regions or with limited production capacity) can pose challenges for inventory management. Selecting reliable suppliers with stable operations can reduce the likelihood of supply chain disruptions.

2. Supplier Reliability and Its Impact on Inventory:

Reduced Safety Stock Requirements: Reliable suppliers who consistently deliver on time and in full enable companies to maintain lower safety stock levels. When companies can trust that their suppliers will fulfill orders as scheduled, they can reduce inventory carrying costs without sacrificing service levels.

Improved Demand-Driven Planning: Reliable suppliers contribute to the effectiveness of demand-driven inventory systems by ensuring a steady flow of goods. This helps companies align inventory levels with actual demand, minimize excess inventory, and avoid stockouts.

Lower Total Cost of Ownership (TCO): High-performing suppliers reduce the need for costly last-minute shipments, rush orders, and inventory stockpiling, which helps companies manage their inventory costs more effectively.

3. Developing a Reliable Supplier Base:

Supplier Selection Process: Choosing suppliers based on performance, reliability, and alignment with demand-driven principles is key to building a reliable supply base. Companies should prioritize suppliers who demonstrate a commitment to on-time delivery, consistent quality, and adaptability to changing demand.

Supplier Development and Support: Investing in supplier development programs, training, and support can help improve supplier performance over time. By offering resources and guidance, companies can help their suppliers implement best practices, which in turn enhances overall supply chain reliability.

Long-Term Contracts and Strategic Partnerships: Establishing long-term contracts or strategic partnerships with key suppliers fosters stability and predictability. Such relationships encourage suppliers to invest in process improvements and innovations that align with the company's demand-driven goals.

Supplier collaboration is a cornerstone of demand-driven inventory management. By building strong relationships with suppliers, companies can reduce lead times, improve forecast accuracy, and achieve greater flexibility in responding to demand fluctuations. Vendor-managed inventory and collaborative planning practices, such as VMI and CPFR, enable suppliers to take an active role in managing inventory, leading to lower stockouts and holding costs. Furthermore, assessing and prioritizing reliable suppliers is essential for maintaining efficient, lean inventory levels and minimizing disruptions. When companies and suppliers work together, they create a more agile and resilient supply chain that aligns with demand-driven principles, ultimately supporting the company's goals of cost efficiency, customer satisfaction, and competitive advantage.

Chapter 13: Technology in Demand-Driven Inventory Management

The growing complexity of supply chains and the evolving needs of businesses have highlighted the critical role technology plays in effective inventory management. Demand-driven inventory management requires a high level of responsiveness and accuracy, which can only be achieved with the help of advanced technologies. By integrating technologies like ERP (Enterprise Resource Planning) systems, IoT (Internet of Things), AI (Artificial Intelligence), and blockchain, companies can ensure inventory levels align with actual demand, reduce inefficiencies, and improve overall supply chain resilience. This chapter explores the role of technology in demand-driven inventory management, focusing on the capabilities of ERP and inventory management systems, emerging technologies, and the importance of data integration and automation.

The Role of ERP and Inventory Management Systems

At the heart of demand-driven inventory management are ERP and inventory management systems. These systems provide a centralized platform for managing inventory data, tracking inventory levels, and coordinating with other business functions, enabling companies to maintain efficient, responsive supply chains. ERP and inventory management systems help synchronize data across departments, optimize reorder points, and ensure accurate inventory records, allowing companies to respond swiftly to demand changes.

1. Core Capabilities of ERP Systems:

Data Centralization and Real-Time Access: ERP systems integrate data from various business functions, including purchasing, sales, production, and distribution, into a single platform. This provides a consolidated view of inventory, enabling real-time tracking of stock levels and inventory movements across the supply chain.

Demand Forecasting and Planning: ERP systems often include demand forecasting tools that use historical data to predict future demand patterns. These forecasts help companies set inventory targets and reorder points, reducing the risk of stockouts and excess inventory.

Inventory Optimization and Replenishment: ERP systems automate inventory replenishment by tracking inventory levels, calculating reorder points, and generating purchase orders when stock levels fall below predetermined thresholds. This automated replenishment ensures that companies maintain optimal stock levels to meet demand without overstocking.

Supply Chain Coordination: By linking different departments and processes, ERP systems improve coordination between suppliers, manufacturers, and distributors. This leads to better alignment of inventory with demand, minimizing lead times and reducing costs associated with excess inventory.

2. Specialized Inventory Management Systems:

While ERP systems offer comprehensive capabilities, specialized inventory management systems focus solely on inventory-related tasks. These systems provide additional functionalities, such as advanced analytics, ABC analysis, and multi-echelon inventory management, which help companies manage inventory at different stages of the supply chain.

Specialized inventory systems allow companies to set specific parameters for different types of inventory (e.g., raw materials, WIP, finished goods) and use advanced optimization algorithms to determine the best inventory levels for each type.

3. The Importance of ERP and Inventory System Integration:

Integrating ERP and inventory management systems with other business software, such as CRM (Customer Relationship Management) and SCM (Supply Chain Management) systems, enhances visibility and data flow across the organization. This integration is crucial for demand-driven inventory management, as it ensures that inventory decisions are based on accurate and up-to-date data from all areas of the business.

Emerging Technologies: IoT, AI, and Blockchain in Inventory Management

Emerging technologies like IoT, AI, and blockchain are transforming demand-driven inventory management by enabling real-time visibility, predictive insights, and secure data sharing. These technologies empower companies to respond more effectively to demand fluctuations, enhance operational efficiency, and mitigate supply chain risks.

1. Internet of Things (IoT):

Real-Time Inventory Tracking: IoT technology enables real-time tracking of inventory through sensors, RFID (Radio-Frequency Identification) tags, and GPS (Global Positioning System) devices. This technology allows companies to monitor inventory levels, location, and condition throughout the supply chain, reducing the risk of stockouts and lost inventory.

Enhanced Inventory Accuracy: IoT sensors help ensure that inventory data is accurate and up-to-date, minimizing discrepancies between recorded and actual stock levels. With IoT-enabled visibility, companies can maintain accurate records of inventory at all times, reducing errors and improving forecasting accuracy.

Predictive Maintenance: IoT can also support demand-driven inventory by enabling predictive maintenance of equipment used in production and logistics. By monitoring equipment performance in real time, companies can proactively address potential issues before they lead to downtime, ensuring that inventory production and distribution processes remain smooth and uninterrupted.

2. Artificial Intelligence (AI) and Machine Learning:

Demand Forecasting and Analytics: AI-powered demand forecasting uses machine learning algorithms to analyze large volumes of data and identify demand patterns with high accuracy. AI can incorporate data from various sources, such as sales trends, economic indicators, and customer behavior, to provide dynamic, demand-driven forecasts that adjust in real time.

Inventory Optimization and Replenishment: AI algorithms can analyze demand variability, lead times, and inventory carrying costs to determine optimal reorder points, safety stock levels, and replenishment quantities. This enables companies to minimize inventory costs while meeting demand requirements.

Demand Sensing: AI can enhance demand sensing by analyzing real-time data, such as sales transactions and social media trends, to identify shifts in demand. By detecting these changes early, companies can adjust their inventory strategies accordingly, ensuring that stock levels align with current demand.

3. Blockchain Technology:

Enhanced Supply Chain Transparency: Blockchain provides a secure and transparent way to track inventory movements and verify

101

transactions across the supply chain. This transparency helps companies monitor inventory flow and detect any potential issues, such as counterfeit products or unauthorized changes, improving inventory accuracy.

Improved Supplier Collaboration: Blockchain enables companies and suppliers to share inventory data on a distributed ledger, allowing both parties to track inventory levels, shipments, and transactions in real time. This fosters collaboration and trust between supply chain partners, reducing lead times and enhancing inventory visibility.

Streamlined Documentation and Compliance: Blockchain can automate the documentation process, ensuring that all inventory-related documents are recorded and accessible to authorized parties. This reduces administrative overhead, improves regulatory compliance, and helps companies avoid costly delays due to missing or incorrect documentation.

The Importance of Data Integration and Automation

To fully leverage the benefits of technology in demand-driven inventory management, companies must integrate data from multiple sources and automate inventory-related processes. Data integration and automation enable seamless information flow, faster decision-making, and a higher level of accuracy in inventory management.

1. Data Integration for Demand-Driven Decisions:

Unified Data Platform: Integrating data from ERP, CRM, SCM, and other systems into a unified platform provides a comprehensive view of inventory across the supply chain. This holistic view helps companies make informed inventory decisions based on real-time demand signals, reducing the likelihood of overstocking or stockouts.

Cross-Functional Collaboration: Data integration facilitates collaboration between departments, such as sales, marketing, and operations, allowing each team to access relevant inventory data. This coordination ensures that inventory strategies align with demand forecasts and business objectives, promoting a demand-driven approach.

Supply Chain Visibility: By integrating data from suppliers, manufacturers, and distributors, companies can gain visibility into inventory levels, lead times, and demand fluctuations throughout the supply chain. This visibility enables companies to make proactive inventory decisions and reduce the impact of supply chain disruptions on inventory.

2. Automation in Inventory Management Processes:

Automated Replenishment and Reordering: Automation reduces manual intervention in replenishment and reordering, allowing companies to respond quickly to demand changes. Automated systems can track inventory levels, detect when stock falls below a certain threshold, and generate purchase orders or transfer requests automatically.

Inventory Counting and Audits: Automated inventory counting systems, such as barcode scanners and RFID readers, streamline the counting process, ensuring that inventory records are accurate and up-to-date. Automated audits reduce human error, improve inventory accuracy, and minimize discrepancies.

Demand-Driven Response Adjustments: Automation can be used to trigger real-time adjustments in response to demand shifts. For example, if a surge in demand for a particular product is detected, an automated system can increase the reorder frequency or raise safety stock levels to ensure sufficient supply.

In today's fast-paced and unpredictable market, technology is a key enabler of demand-driven inventory management. ERP and specialized inventory management systems provide the foundation for centralized data, streamlined processes, and accurate inventory tracking, while emerging technologies like IoT, AI, and blockchain take inventory management to new levels of visibility, intelligence, and security. By integrating data across departments and automating inventory processes, companies can align inventory with demand more effectively, reduce costs, and enhance customer satisfaction. As technology continues to advance, companies that adopt these tools and practices will be better positioned to navigate the complexities of modern supply chains and thrive in a demand-driven environment.

Chapter 14: Data Analytics and Inventory Management

Data analytics has become a cornerstone of demand-driven inventory management, allowing companies to make smarter, data-informed decisions that improve efficiency, reduce costs, and enhance customer satisfaction. By leveraging analytics tools for demand forecasting, replenishment, and inventory optimization, companies can gain a clearer understanding of demand patterns, identify optimization opportunities, and respond quickly to fluctuations in the market. This chapter explores the types of data used in demand-driven inventory management, key analytics tools, and the insights that data analytics offers for making informed inventory decisions.

Types of Data Used in Demand-Driven Inventory Management

Demand-driven inventory management relies on a wide range of data to achieve accurate demand forecasting, efficient replenishment, and effective optimization. The data used can be classified into several categories, each of which provides unique insights into inventory needs and demand fluctuations.

1. Historical Sales Data:

Historical sales data is one of the most valuable datasets for demand-driven inventory management. This data provides insight into past demand trends, seasonality, and buying patterns, which can be used to forecast future demand and determine optimal stock levels.

By analyzing past sales, companies can identify patterns and adjust inventory levels to account for anticipated demand surges or declines.

2. Real-Time Sales and Point-of-Sale (POS) Data:

Real-time sales data, often gathered from POS systems, allows companies to monitor current demand and respond quickly to changes.

This is particularly useful for fast-moving products, where immediate adjustments to inventory are needed to prevent stockouts or overstock situations.

Real-time sales data is critical for demand sensing, helping companies detect sudden demand shifts and make agile inventory adjustments.

3. Market and Economic Data:

External market data, such as economic indicators, competitive actions, and consumer trends, provides a broader context for demand patterns. Economic data, such as interest rates, inflation, and consumer confidence, can impact purchasing behaviors and overall demand for products.

Analyzing this data helps companies understand external factors that could influence demand and inventory needs, enabling proactive adjustments.

4. Inventory Movement and Transaction Data:

Transactional data related to inventory movements, such as receipts, shipments, and returns, allows companies to track inventory flow throughout the supply chain. This data provides insight into lead times, inventory turnover, and the efficiency of internal processes.

Transactional data also helps identify bottlenecks or inefficiencies in the supply chain, allowing for process improvements and better inventory positioning.

5. Supplier and Lead Time Data:

Supplier data, including historical lead times, delivery accuracy, and reliability, is essential for planning and replenishment. Understanding supplier performance allows companies to set realistic lead times and adjust inventory levels accordingly.

Supplier data also helps identify high-risk suppliers that may require closer monitoring or contingency planning to avoid disruptions.

6. Customer and Demand Signals:

Data from customer orders, inquiries, and interactions (such as social media sentiment or website traffic) provides early signals of changing demand. This data is valuable for demand shaping and helps companies anticipate shifts in customer preferences or expectations.

By integrating customer demand signals into inventory planning, companies can create a more responsive, customer-focused inventory strategy.

Analytics Tools for Demand Forecasting, Replenishment, and Optimization

Analytics tools play a central role in transforming raw data into actionable insights for demand-driven inventory management. Various tools and techniques can be used to improve demand forecasting, streamline replenishment, and optimize inventory levels to match demand patterns.

1. Demand Forecasting Tools:

Time Series Analysis: Time series analysis is commonly used in demand forecasting to analyze historical demand data and identify patterns such as trends, seasonality, and cyclical behaviors. Techniques like moving averages, exponential smoothing, and ARIMA (Auto-Regressive Integrated Moving Average) are used to predict future demand based on past trends.

Machine Learning and Predictive Analytics: Machine learning algorithms use historical and real-time data to detect demand patterns and generate predictive models. These models can incorporate multiple variables, such as market trends, weather patterns, and economic indicators, to improve forecast accuracy.

Demand Sensing: Demand sensing tools use real-time sales data and customer demand signals to make short-term demand predictions. This approach allows companies to respond quickly to sudden demand changes, improving forecast accuracy and reducing the risk of stockouts or overstocking.

2. Inventory Replenishment Tools:

Reorder Point (ROP) and Safety Stock Calculations: Replenishment tools calculate reorder points and safety stock levels based on demand variability and lead time. These calculations ensure that inventory is restocked before reaching critical levels, helping to maintain service levels while minimizing excess stock.

Automated Replenishment Systems: Automated systems track inventory levels in real time and generate purchase orders when inventory falls below predetermined thresholds. This automation streamlines the replenishment process, ensuring that inventory levels are maintained efficiently without manual intervention.

Multi-Echelon Inventory Optimization (MEIO): MEIO tools optimize inventory levels across multiple stages or locations within the supply chain, considering factors like lead times, demand variability, and inventory carrying costs. This approach reduces overall inventory levels while maintaining service levels across the entire supply chain.

3. Inventory Optimization Tools:

ABC Analysis: ABC analysis categorizes inventory based on value or demand frequency, allowing companies to prioritize high-value or fast-moving items for tighter control. This technique helps companies focus resources on the most critical items while managing less critical stock at a lower cost.

Economic Order Quantity (EOQ): EOQ is a mathematical model that calculates the ideal order quantity to minimize ordering and carrying costs. By balancing these costs, EOQ helps companies determine the most cost-effective quantity for replenishing inventory.

Simulation Models: Simulation tools model various inventory scenarios, such as demand spikes, lead time delays, or supply chain disruptions, to evaluate how these scenarios would impact inventory levels. These tools allow companies to test different strategies and choose the most effective approach for their inventory needs.

Insights Derived from Data for Better Decision-Making

The insights derived from data analytics enable companies to make better, more informed decisions in demand-driven inventory management. By understanding demand patterns, identifying risks, and uncovering optimization opportunities, companies can achieve a more efficient, responsive, and cost-effective inventory strategy.

1. Improved Forecast Accuracy:

Accurate demand forecasts are essential for minimizing stockouts, reducing excess inventory, and maintaining high service levels. With analytics tools, companies can create demand forecasts that reflect real-time data and consider external factors, resulting in more reliable predictions.

Improved forecast accuracy leads to better inventory planning, ensuring that inventory levels align with actual demand rather than relying on historical trends alone.

2. Better Inventory Positioning:

Data analytics helps companies determine the optimal locations for holding inventory, considering factors like demand variability, lead times, and transportation costs. By strategically positioning inventory, companies can reduce lead times and respond more quickly to demand changes.

Positioning inventory closer to demand sources also minimizes transportation costs and reduces the risk of supply chain disruptions.

3. Enhanced Replenishment and Ordering:

By using replenishment tools and analytics, companies can set reorder points and safety stock levels that reflect current demand and lead times. This ensures that inventory is replenished at the right time, reducing carrying costs and minimizing the risk of stockouts.

Analytics also allow companies to automate replenishment, freeing up resources for higher-value activities and ensuring consistent stock levels.

4. Cost Reduction and Efficiency Gains:

Inventory optimization tools help companies identify opportunities to reduce inventory-related costs, such as carrying costs, ordering costs, and stockout costs. By analyzing inventory data, companies can find ways to reduce excess stock, streamline ordering, and improve service levels.

Efficiency gains from analytics extend beyond cost savings; by reducing excess inventory and minimizing lead times, companies can achieve a more efficient, demand-responsive inventory management approach.

5. Risk Management and Contingency Planning:

Data analytics helps companies identify risks related to demand variability, lead time fluctuations, and supplier performance. By understanding these risks, companies can establish contingency plans, such as buffer stocks or alternative suppliers, to mitigate potential disruptions.

Proactive risk management based on data insights helps companies navigate uncertainties, improving resilience and reducing the impact of unexpected events.

6. Strategic Decision-Making and Demand Shaping:

With the insights provided by analytics, companies can make strategic decisions regarding product promotions, pricing adjustments, and inventory levels to influence demand patterns. Demand shaping allows companies to align inventory levels with anticipated demand shifts, enhancing customer satisfaction and reducing excess stock.

Strategic use of analytics in demand shaping also allows companies to identify profitable opportunities, such as expanding product lines or targeting new customer segments, to drive growth and maximize inventory value.

Data analytics is essential for effective demand-driven inventory management, providing the tools and insights needed to forecast demand accurately, replenish inventory efficiently, and optimize stock levels. By leveraging historical sales data, real-time demand signals, and external market indicators, companies can develop a responsive, data-informed approach to inventory management that aligns with market demand and minimizes costs. Analytics tools, from demand forecasting and replenishment automation to inventory optimization models, empower companies to make strategic inventory decisions that enhance service levels, improve operational efficiency, and mitigate risks. As data analytics continues to evolve, companies that invest in these tools and integrate data-driven practices into their inventory strategies will be well-positioned to succeed in an increasingly competitive market.

Chapter 15: Managing Inventory in an Omnichannel Environment

In today's retail landscape, managing inventory across multiple channels—whether online, in-store, or through third-party marketplaces—has become essential as businesses adopt an omnichannel approach to meet customer expectations for seamless shopping experiences. Omnichannel inventory management integrates stock across all platforms, allowing customers to order and receive products through their preferred channels, whether online or in-store. However, this approach brings unique challenges, such as demand variability across channels, the need for real-time inventory visibility, and complex fulfillment processes. This chapter explores these challenges, examines the impact of omnichannel demand on inventory strategies, and discusses best practices for achieving inventory visibility and optimizing fulfillment in an omnichannel environment.

Challenges of Managing Inventory Across Channels

Successfully managing inventory in an omnichannel environment requires overcoming significant hurdles to ensure that stock is available where and when customers need it. These challenges are heightened by the complex interplay of different channels, fluctuating customer demand, and logistical constraints.

1. Inventory Fragmentation Across Channels:

Inventory fragmentation occurs when stock is dispersed across multiple sales channels (e.g., online, in-store, or wholesale) and managed separately. This approach often leads to inefficiencies, as excess inventory may accumulate in one channel while another experiences stockouts.

Fragmented inventory management can also make it difficult to optimize stock levels, leading to higher carrying costs and an inability to respond quickly to demand fluctuations.

2. Demand Variability and Forecasting Challenges:

In an omnichannel environment, customer demand can vary widely across channels, making it challenging to forecast accurately. Demand for online purchases might surge during promotional events, while in-store sales may spike in specific regions or seasons.

Traditional forecasting methods may not be sufficient to capture these variations, requiring more sophisticated models that account for channel-specific demand drivers and seasonality.

3. Complex Fulfillment Requirements:

Omnichannel fulfillment models, such as buy online, pick up in-store (BOPIS), ship from store, and same-day delivery, require complex coordination of inventory, orders, and logistics. Each fulfillment method has its own requirements and cost implications.

Managing inventory to support diverse fulfillment options adds a layer of complexity, as companies must ensure that each channel has adequate stock to meet demand while minimizing excess inventory.

4. Maintaining Real-Time Inventory Visibility:

Real-time inventory visibility is crucial for omnichannel success, as it allows businesses to update inventory levels across channels and fulfill orders accurately. Without real-time data, companies risk accepting orders for out-of-stock items or missing sales opportunities due to stock unavailability.

Achieving this level of visibility can be challenging, especially for companies with legacy systems or fragmented data sources that hinder real-time information sharing.

5. Balancing Service Levels and Cost Efficiency:

Omnichannel environments require companies to balance high service levels with cost efficiency. Meeting customer expectations for fast and flexible fulfillment can lead to higher costs in inventory handling, shipping, and last-mile delivery.

Finding the right balance between service levels and cost containment is critical, as companies must deliver a positive customer experience while managing the financial impact of omnichannel operations.

Omnichannel Demand and Its Impact on Inventory Strategies

Omnichannel demand creates unique requirements for inventory strategies, as companies must consider the distinct demand patterns and customer expectations associated with each channel. To effectively manage omnichannel inventory, companies must adapt their strategies to meet these demands while maintaining a unified view of inventory.

1. Unified Inventory Approach:

A unified inventory approach treats inventory as a single pool that can be allocated to any channel based on demand. By centralizing inventory management, companies can optimize stock allocation and reduce the risk of stockouts in one channel while holding excess inventory in another.

This approach allows companies to respond more flexibly to demand fluctuations across channels, reallocating stock as needed to maximize availability and reduce costs.

2. Dynamic Reallocation Based on Demand Patterns:

In an omnichannel setup, demand can shift rapidly between channels due to promotions, customer preferences, or seasonal trends. Dynamic reallocation allows companies to move stock from one channel to another in response to these shifts.

For example, if demand spikes in the online channel, inventory allocated to brick-and-mortar stores can be redirected to fulfill online orders. This agility is essential for maintaining service levels in an omnichannel environment.

3. Buffer Stock and Safety Stock Considerations:

Buffer stock and safety stock are essential for handling demand uncertainty in omnichannel environments. However, these stock levels must be carefully calibrated to avoid overstocking, which increases carrying costs, or understocking, which risks stockouts.

Determining the right level of buffer stock for each channel can be challenging, but it is necessary to prevent service disruptions and ensure high availability across all sales platforms.

4. Flexible Fulfillment Models:

To meet customer expectations for fast and flexible fulfillment, companies may adopt multiple fulfillment models, such as BOPIS, ship from store, and warehouse-to-customer shipping. Each model has different inventory requirements and cost implications.

Developing flexible fulfillment models that allow inventory to be pulled from various locations as needed can improve efficiency and speed while reducing the overall inventory burden.

5. Forecasting for Cross-Channel Promotions:

Cross-channel promotions, where discounts or marketing campaigns span online and in-store channels, create spikes in demand that must be accurately forecasted. For example, a Black Friday sale may drive online traffic as well as in-store footfall, requiring increased inventory across all channels.

Effective cross-channel promotion forecasting can prevent stockouts and ensure inventory availability where it is most needed, while minimizing excess stock.

Inventory Visibility and Fulfillment in Omnichannel Setups

Real-time inventory visibility and efficient fulfillment processes are fundamental to successful omnichannel inventory management. These capabilities ensure that companies can meet customer expectations for fast, accurate, and flexible order fulfillment while optimizing inventory levels.

1. Importance of Real-Time Inventory Visibility:

Real-time inventory visibility is essential for omnichannel operations, allowing companies to monitor stock levels across all locations and channels. With accurate visibility, companies can avoid stockouts, reduce excess inventory, and fulfill orders accurately.

Real-time visibility also enhances decision-making, as it provides data-driven insights into demand patterns, inventory turnover, and fulfillment efficiency, enabling proactive inventory management.

2. Integrating Inventory Management Systems:

Achieving real-time visibility requires integrated inventory management systems that connect all channels and fulfillment centers. Enterprise Resource Planning (ERP) and Warehouse Management Systems (WMS) can be synchronized to provide a centralized view of inventory.

Integration ensures that inventory data is updated across systems as stock moves through the supply chain, providing a unified view of availability and enabling accurate order fulfillment.

3. Role of Distributed Order Management (DOM):

Distributed Order Management (DOM) systems play a key role in omnichannel fulfillment, as they allocate orders to the most suitable location based on inventory availability, proximity to the customer, and cost considerations.

DOM enables efficient fulfillment by optimizing the sourcing of products, reducing shipping costs, and ensuring timely delivery. This system is particularly valuable for companies with multiple fulfillment centers and sales channels.

4. Fulfillment Strategies:

Buy Online, Pick Up In-Store (BOPIS): BOPIS allows customers to purchase products online and collect them from a nearby store. This model reduces shipping costs and supports customer convenience but requires accurate stock data to prevent stockouts.

Ship from Store: In the ship-from-store model, physical stores function as mini-distribution centers, shipping online orders directly to customers. This model can reduce delivery times and optimize inventory usage across the network.

Same-Day and Next-Day Delivery: Offering same-day or next-day delivery requires fast, accurate inventory management and efficient order processing. Companies may need to hold buffer stock in local fulfillment centers or use third-party logistics providers to meet these expectations.

5. Managing Returns Across Channels:

Returns are a common aspect of omnichannel retail, and managing returns across channels can be complex. Customers may buy online and return in-store or vice versa, requiring companies to track returns and reintegrate products into inventory efficiently.

An effective returns management process reduces costs, improves customer satisfaction, and minimizes excess inventory by quickly restocking returned items where they are most needed.

6. Enhancing Customer Experience through Inventory Visibility:

Customers expect to know whether a product is in stock and available for their preferred fulfillment option (e.g., delivery, pickup) before they make a purchase. Real-time inventory visibility on websites, apps, and in-store systems enhances the customer experience by providing accurate availability information.

Improved visibility also reduces the likelihood of order cancellations due to stockouts, which can harm customer satisfaction and loyalty.

Conclusion

Managing inventory in an omnichannel environment is both challenging and essential in today's retail landscape. As businesses operate across multiple channels and offer diverse fulfillment options, maintaining efficient inventory management becomes crucial for meeting customer expectations and optimizing operational costs. The challenges of omnichannel inventory management—such as demand variability, complex fulfillment requirements, and the need for real-time visibility—require a strategic approach that includes unified inventory management, dynamic reallocation, and advanced inventory visibility tools.

By integrating inventory systems, adopting flexible fulfillment models, and leveraging real-time data, companies can achieve a responsive and efficient omnichannel inventory strategy. This approach not only enhances the customer experience but also enables companies to navigate the complexities of multi-channel operations, reduce costs, and build a more agile, demand-driven inventory management process. As the retail landscape continues to evolve, companies that master omnichannel inventory management will be better equipped to meet the demands of a diverse, digitally-connected customer base.

Chapter 16: Demand-Driven Inventory in E-Commerce

E-commerce has transformed the way consumers shop, leading to unique challenges for inventory management. Unlike traditional retail, e-commerce operates in a high-velocity environment where demand can fluctuate dramatically, influenced by promotions, seasonality, and consumer trends. Managing inventory in e-commerce involves balancing the need for product availability with cost control while meeting customer expectations for speed and flexibility. This chapter explores the specific inventory challenges in e-commerce, strategies for managing online demand surges and seasonality, and inventory strategies tailored to e-commerce fulfillment models.

Specific Inventory Challenges in E-Commerce

The rapid pace and unpredictability of e-commerce present several challenges to effective inventory management. Understanding these challenges is essential to create a responsive, demand-driven inventory system.

1. High Demand Volatility and Short Product Life Cycles:

E-commerce demand is highly volatile, often driven by trends, promotions, and social media influence. This can lead to sudden spikes or drops in demand, making forecasting difficult.

Many e-commerce products have shorter life cycles, particularly in industries like fashion and electronics, where seasonal or technological changes render products obsolete quickly.

2. Order Fulfillment Expectations and Fast Shipping:

E-commerce customers expect fast and flexible fulfillment, including same-day or next-day delivery, which requires inventory to be readily available and in proximity to the customer.

Meeting these expectations while managing costs is challenging, as it involves holding inventory closer to demand points, often in multiple distribution centers.

3. Returns Management and Reverse Logistics:

E-commerce experiences higher return rates compared to brick-and-mortar stores, especially in categories like apparel, where fit and style vary by customer.

Effective reverse logistics is necessary to manage returns efficiently, as returned items must be inspected, repackaged, and restocked promptly to minimize the financial impact on inventory.

4. Stockout and Overstock Risks:

Stockouts in e-commerce can lead to lost sales and dissatisfied customers, as customers can easily switch to competitors.

Overstocking, on the other hand, ties up capital and increases holding costs, especially for products with limited shelf life or high obsolescence risk.

5. Integration Across Multiple Sales Channels:

Many e-commerce businesses operate across multiple platforms, such as their own website, third-party marketplaces (like Amazon and eBay), and social media.

Managing inventory across these channels requires integration to ensure that inventory visibility is synchronized and that stock levels are updated in real-time.

Managing Online Demand Surges and Seasonality

E-commerce demand surges and seasonality require proactive strategies to ensure that inventory levels align with expected demand while minimizing waste. Demand surges are common during holidays, major sales events, and promotional periods, while seasonal demand varies by industry and product category.

1. Forecasting for Demand Surges and Seasonal Peaks:

Accurate demand forecasting is essential for planning inventory for peak periods. Forecasting models that incorporate historical data, seasonal trends, and external factors (like holiday promotions or marketing campaigns) help to anticipate demand spikes.

Advanced analytics, such as machine learning, can improve forecasting accuracy by analyzing patterns in past demand and adjusting predictions in real-time as new data comes in.

2. Safety Stock for Peak Periods:

E-commerce businesses often hold extra inventory, or safety stock, to cover unexpected demand increases during peak seasons.

For instance, a retailer might maintain higher safety stock leading up to Black Friday, Cyber Monday, or holiday shopping seasons, where demand traditionally surges.

3. Pre-positioning Inventory Near Demand Centers:

To meet high demand during surges, e-commerce companies may pre-position inventory close to major demand centers or in specific geographic regions.

This strategy reduces shipping times, lowers costs, and ensures inventory is readily available to meet sudden increases in local demand.

4. Dynamic Reallocation of Inventory:

Dynamic reallocation enables businesses to shift inventory between fulfillment centers in response to demand changes. For example, if one region is experiencing a demand surge, inventory from slower regions can be rerouted to meet this demand.

Real-time inventory data and distributed order management systems are essential to make these adjustments quickly and accurately.

5. Inventory and Fulfillment Strategies for Promotional Events:

E-commerce retailers often run flash sales or promotional events that generate significant demand within a short time frame. Preparing for these events involves adjusting inventory levels, setting up special fulfillment processes, and managing order capacity to avoid bottlenecks.

Promotions often require flexible inventory policies, allowing companies to restock popular items quickly if they sell out or to liquidate slow-moving stock at reduced prices to avoid carrying excess inventory after the event.

Inventory Strategies for E-Commerce Fulfillment Models

E-commerce has driven the development of diverse fulfillment models, each with distinct inventory management requirements. Businesses can enhance their responsiveness and efficiency by aligning inventory strategies with their chosen fulfillment models.

1. Fulfillment by Warehouse and Distribution Centers:

Centralized Warehousing: A centralized approach consolidates inventory in a single or limited number of distribution centers. This strategy can reduce storage costs but may increase shipping times and costs for customers located far from these centers.

Decentralized Warehousing: In contrast, a decentralized model distributes inventory across multiple regional warehouses, bringing products closer to customers and reducing shipping times and costs. This approach requires a more complex inventory management system to balance stock levels across multiple locations.

2. Drop Shipping:

In a drop shipping model, inventory is held by the supplier or manufacturer rather than the retailer. This allows e-commerce businesses to offer a wide range of products without holding inventory, reducing carrying costs and risk.

However, drop shipping limits inventory control, as the business relies on the supplier's stock availability and fulfillment speed, which can impact customer satisfaction if not managed carefully.

3. Fulfillment by Third-Party Providers:

Many e-commerce companies partner with third-party logistics (3PL) providers, such as Amazon FBA (Fulfillment by Amazon), to manage their inventory and fulfillment operations. These providers offer scalable fulfillment solutions, particularly useful during peak seasons.

Using a 3PL provider requires integration between the e-commerce platform and the provider's system to synchronize inventory levels and order data, ensuring seamless fulfillment.

4. Buy Online, Pick Up In-Store (BOPIS):

BOPIS allows customers to purchase online and collect items in a physical store, bridging the gap between e-commerce and brick-and-mortar retail. This model requires real-time inventory tracking to confirm availability and streamline order fulfillment.

BOPIS can reduce shipping costs, improve customer satisfaction, and leverage existing store inventory, but it requires robust inventory management systems to keep track of online and in-store stock.

5. Just-in-Time (JIT) Inventory for High-Demand Items:

A JIT approach minimizes inventory by synchronizing stock replenishment with demand. This model works well for high-demand items with predictable turnover, reducing carrying costs and enhancing inventory agility.

However, JIT requires a high level of coordination with suppliers to ensure timely replenishment, as any disruption can lead to stockouts and lost sales.

Technology for E-Commerce Inventory Management

Advanced technology plays a crucial role in addressing e-commerce inventory challenges and optimizing demand-driven inventory management.

1. Real-Time Inventory Tracking:

Real-time tracking systems provide up-to-the-minute data on stock levels, helping e-commerce businesses manage inventory across multiple warehouses and sales channels. This enables businesses to respond quickly to demand changes and avoid stockouts.

Technologies like RFID and IoT sensors further enhance visibility, especially for items that move frequently between locations or have high turnover rates.

2. Automated Replenishment and Order Management:

Automated replenishment systems analyze demand patterns to forecast when inventory needs to be reordered, reducing manual intervention and ensuring consistent availability.

Order management systems (OMS) play a critical role in e-commerce, directing orders to the most suitable fulfillment center based on factors like inventory levels, location, and shipping cost.

3. Predictive Analytics and Machine Learning for Demand Forecasting:

Machine learning algorithms analyze historical data, market trends, and other variables to predict demand more accurately. Predictive analytics can identify patterns in customer behavior, enabling more responsive inventory planning for future sales.

These technologies also support demand sensing, adjusting forecasts in real-time to account for factors like social media trends or sudden spikes in interest, which is invaluable in fast-paced e-commerce environments.

4. Advanced Warehouse Management Systems (WMS):

A robust WMS is essential for tracking inventory within and across warehouses. E-commerce companies use WMS solutions to streamline receiving, putaway, picking, and packing processes, minimizing the time and labor required for order fulfillment.

WMS software can integrate with other systems, such as ERP and OMS, to synchronize inventory data and ensure that stock is accurately reflected across all channels.

5. Customer-Facing Inventory Transparency:

E-commerce customers increasingly expect transparency around inventory availability. Businesses can use technology to display accurate stock levels on their websites, improving the customer experience and reducing the likelihood of stockouts.

Transparency also enables features like back-in-stock notifications, which allow customers to request updates for out-of-stock items, helping companies manage demand for popular products.

Demand-driven inventory management is essential for success in the e-commerce space, where demand surges, seasonality, and high customer expectations present significant challenges. To meet these challenges, e-commerce companies must adopt inventory strategies that balance availability and cost-efficiency while leveraging technology to enhance accuracy and responsiveness.

By understanding the specific demands of e-commerce, managing inventory across multiple channels, and using technology to forecast, track, and replenish stock, companies can create an agile and demand-driven inventory management system. This approach not only reduces costs and minimizes waste but also improves the overall customer experience—an essential factor in achieving long-term success in the competitive world of e-commerce.

Chapter 17: Seasonal Demand and Promotional Planning

Seasonal demand and promotional events are integral aspects of inventory management, particularly for businesses dealing with significant fluctuations throughout the year. Effective planning for these periods ensures that inventory levels are optimized, minimizing both stockouts and excess stock. This chapter discusses strategies for planning around seasonal demand and promotions, balancing inventory during peak and off-peak times, and managing inventory for holiday and special events.

Understanding Seasonal Demand and Promotions

Seasonal demand refers to predictable fluctuations in consumer demand based on the time of year, such as back-to-school season, holiday shopping, or summer sports gear. Promotions, on the other hand, are usually time-specific events designed to boost sales, often coinciding with holidays or other peak periods.

Types of Seasonal Demand: Demand can vary by industry, such as holiday gift items in retail, summer travel gear, or winter sports equipment. Understanding the specific demand patterns for a business's product line is crucial.

Impact of Promotions on Demand: Promotions often generate a sharp increase in demand within a short timeframe. This is particularly true during annual events like Black Friday, Cyber Monday, and other holiday sales. Promotional demand can be more difficult to forecast, as it often depends on marketing success, competitive offers, and market trends.

How to Plan for Seasonal Demand and Promotions

Effective planning for seasonal demand and promotions involves forecasting demand accurately, aligning inventory levels with anticipated demand, and implementing flexible strategies to adapt to real-time changes. Here are some key steps:

1. Accurate Demand Forecasting:

Historical Data Analysis: Historical sales data helps identify demand trends from previous seasons. Using data from multiple years provides insights into recurring demand patterns, helping managers make better predictions.

Market Trends and Influencers: For industries influenced by fashion, technology trends, or external factors, analyzing current market trends can refine forecasts. Social media monitoring and trend analysis tools can help identify emerging demands.

Collaborative Forecasting with Key Stakeholders: Collaborating with suppliers, distributors, and sales teams ensures forecasts are aligned with expected demand and that any potential disruptions or changes are accounted for.

2. Inventory Build-Up Strategy:

Staggered Inventory Build-Up: Gradually increasing inventory in the weeks leading up to a peak season allows companies to avoid a sudden influx of stock, reducing the risk of storage constraints.

Pre-positioning Inventory: Placing inventory in regional distribution centers closer to demand areas shortens delivery times and improves customer satisfaction. This approach is especially useful for seasonal items, which tend to be in high demand for a short period.

Setting Safety Stock for Seasonal Items: Safety stock levels should be adjusted for peak periods to minimize the risk of stockouts, particularly for high-demand items. This involves understanding the lead time and variability in demand for seasonal products.

3. Flexible Inventory Management During Promotions:

Demand Sensing: Using real-time data to track demand during promotions allows businesses to respond quickly to sales patterns. Demand sensing can help adjust inventory levels and replenishment rates to better meet actual demand.

Dynamic Replenishment Models: Rather than relying solely on pre-season inventory, dynamic replenishment allows for adjustments based on actual sales trends as the season progresses. For example, increasing restocks on popular items can help avoid stockouts while reducing restocks for slower-moving products.

Cross-Functional Planning and Communication: Aligning marketing, sales, and supply chain teams ensures that inventory plans match promotional goals. Marketing insights about expected customer interest can help supply chain managers prepare inventory accurately.

Balancing Inventory for Peak Seasons and Off-Seasons

Balancing inventory during peak and off-peak periods is crucial to avoid the costs associated with overstock and understock. Here are some strategies to manage these challenges effectively:

1. Differentiated Inventory Strategies for Peaks and Lulls:

Seasonal Stock Adjustments: During peak seasons, inventory should focus on high-demand items while maintaining minimal stock of off-season items. For example, in winter, retailers might reduce summer inventory to free up space for winter products.

Lean Inventory in Off-Seasons: In slower periods, reducing inventory levels can lower storage costs and minimize the risk of holding obsolete stock. For example, after the holiday season, companies might hold only essential stock to avoid tying up capital in excess inventory.

2. Inventory Pooling for Flexibility:

Shared Inventory Pools Across Channels: Sharing inventory across different channels (e.g., online and retail) can help distribute stock more efficiently. This approach enables managers to adjust inventory levels based on real-time demand fluctuations.

Regional Redistribution of Stock: Businesses with multiple warehouses or stores can shift excess stock from low-demand areas to regions with higher demand. This helps avoid stockouts in peak areas while minimizing inventory waste in lower-demand locations.

3. Vendor and Supplier Collaboration:

Flexible Supplier Agreements: Agreements that allow for flexible order quantities or delivery schedules can help companies respond quickly to changing demand patterns. Vendors who understand the business's seasonality can work together to streamline lead times and accommodate last-minute adjustments.

Consignment Inventory: Consignment models, where suppliers retain ownership of inventory until it is sold, are helpful for seasonal items. This arrangement can minimize financial risk during off-peak periods by reducing the holding cost for the retailer.

Inventory Management During Holiday and Special Events

Holidays and special events require detailed planning, as these periods often see sharp demand spikes over short timeframes. Efficient management during these times involves optimizing stock, enhancing fulfillment capacity, and preparing for potential supply chain disruptions.

1. Pre-Season Inventory Build-Up for Holiday Periods:

Lead-Time Adjustments for Early Ordering: Ordering inventory earlier than usual accounts for potential delays or high demand from suppliers during peak seasons. This is especially relevant when sourcing from international suppliers who might also experience demand spikes.

Increasing Safety Stock Levels: For the most popular holiday items, increasing safety stock provides a buffer against unexpected demand surges. The level of safety stock should consider the time to replenish, potential delays, and the financial impact of stockouts during peak sales periods.

2. Enhancing Fulfillment Capacity and Staffing:

Warehouse Optimization for Faster Picking and Packing: Warehouses should be configured to streamline order picking, packing, and shipping. Using technology like automated picking or advanced WMS (Warehouse Management Systems) can increase efficiency during peak periods.

Seasonal Staffing and Cross-Training: Hiring seasonal staff and cross-training regular employees in different tasks allows companies to handle higher order volumes without compromising fulfillment speed. Cross-trained employees can help manage bottlenecks by filling roles as demand shifts.

3. Preparing for Return and Reverse Logistics:

Forecasting Return Rates and Allocating Space for Returns: Peak season returns, particularly after holidays, often require additional space and staff to process returns efficiently. By forecasting return rates, businesses can allocate resources to manage reverse logistics without delaying new orders.

Implementing Clear Return Policies: Clear, customer-friendly return policies, such as free returns for holiday purchases, can enhance customer satisfaction. However, setting boundaries for these policies helps mitigate the risk of excessive returns post-holiday.

4. Promotional Event Planning:

Flash Sales and Limited-Time Offers: Flash sales often lead to rapid inventory turnover, requiring pre-planned stock levels to ensure availability. Planning for these events includes forecasting the impact on demand, setting aside inventory for specific items, and planning for potential stockouts.

Discount Strategies for Post-Holiday Inventory Clearance: Inventory that remains after peak seasons can be discounted to free up storage space and reduce holding costs. Clearance strategies also prevent excess stock from becoming obsolete by the next peak season.

Leveraging Technology for Seasonal Inventory Management

Technology is essential for tracking, forecasting, and managing seasonal inventory effectively. Here's how different technologies can support seasonal demand and promotional planning:

1. Advanced Forecasting Tools:

Demand Forecasting Software: Software tools that incorporate machine learning and predictive analytics help improve forecast accuracy by analyzing historical data, external factors, and seasonal trends.

Real-Time Inventory Monitoring: Real-time data collection provides accurate stock levels, allowing businesses to make timely adjustments based on demand fluctuations.

2. Warehouse Management Systems (WMS):

Automated Inventory Control: A WMS helps optimize warehouse layout, picking, and restocking processes to ensure efficient operations during high-demand seasons.

Cross-Channel Fulfillment Coordination: For companies with online and physical stores, a WMS enables inventory coordination across channels, minimizing stockouts and ensuring customer satisfaction across all platforms.

3. Collaboration Tools for Supplier Coordination:

Supplier Portals and Communication Platforms: Technology enables real-time communication with suppliers, allowing businesses to share forecasts and adjust orders as needed to respond to seasonal changes.

Vendor-Managed Inventory (VMI): In a VMI arrangement, suppliers manage inventory replenishment for retailers based on shared sales data. This minimizes the retailer's risk while ensuring adequate stock during peak seasons.

4. Data Analytics for Demand Sensing and Adjustments:

Predictive Analytics for Real-Time Demand Sensing: By analyzing sales data and consumer behavior in real-time, predictive analytics can signal demand shifts early, allowing companies to adapt inventory levels accordingly.

Inventory Optimization Algorithms: Optimization tools help determine the most efficient stock levels to balance demand across regions and warehouses, avoiding overstock or stockouts during seasonal peaks.

Managing seasonal demand and promotions is essential for maintaining an efficient and responsive inventory system. Through accurate forecasting, strategic inventory build-up, flexible supplier relationships, and robust technology, companies can better align their inventory management with seasonal fluctuations. By preparing for peak seasons and managing inventory flows throughout the year, businesses can minimize stockouts, reduce excess inventory costs, and maximize profitability—ultimately delivering a seamless customer experience even during high-demand periods.

Chapter 18: Reverse Logistics and Inventory Reclamation

As e-commerce and customer expectations for flexible return policies grow, reverse logistics and inventory reclamation have become essential aspects of modern inventory management. Efficiently managing product returns, reclaiming inventory value, and mitigating associated costs are all crucial in this process. This chapter explores the impact of reverse logistics on inventory levels, cost implications, and strategies for maximizing the value of returned items through repurposing or reselling.

Understanding Reverse Logistics and Its Importance

Reverse logistics involves the process of moving goods from the customer back to the seller or manufacturer, typically for returns, repairs, refurbishment, recycling, or disposal. This process can be complex, requiring careful coordination to manage the flow of goods in reverse and reclaiming inventory value where possible. For businesses, handling returns efficiently has both operational and financial benefits, as well as a significant impact on customer satisfaction and loyalty.

Definition of Reverse Logistics: Reverse logistics includes all activities related to returns management, which may encompass inspection, repackaging, repair, or disposal.

Growing Importance in E-commerce: With e-commerce on the rise, return rates are higher compared to brick-and-mortar retail. For some categories, such as fashion, return rates can exceed 30%. Efficient reverse logistics helps reduce the impact on inventory costs and improves profit margins by effectively managing these returns.

Impact on Customer Experience: A well-structured returns process not only reduces costs but also enhances customer loyalty by providing a smooth, hassle-free return experience.

Handling Returns and Reverse Logistics Efficiently

Managing reverse logistics efficiently involves streamlining returns processing, establishing a clear returns policy, and implementing technology to optimize the reverse flow of inventory. Here are several key considerations and best practices:

1. Developing a Clear and Customer-Friendly Returns Policy:

Transparency in Return Policies: Clear, upfront communication regarding return conditions (timeframe, condition of returned items, refund or store credit options) can reduce processing time and minimize the likelihood of returns abuse.

Simplifying the Return Process: Offering pre-paid return labels, drop-off points, or pick-up services can improve customer satisfaction and simplify reverse logistics.

Setting Return Criteria: Establishing strict criteria for what constitutes an acceptable return helps avoid processing defective or worn items unnecessarily, saving costs on inspecting and reconditioning products.

2. Streamlining the Returns Processing System:

Centralized Return Centers: Directing returns to a central facility speeds up the processing, inspection, and sorting of returned products, allowing companies to reintroduce sellable items to inventory quickly.

Efficient Handling Procedures: Returns should be categorized (reusable, repairable, recyclable, disposable) as soon as they are received to avoid clutter and bottlenecks in the warehouse.

Technology Integration for Reverse Logistics: Integrating a Warehouse Management System (WMS) or a specialized returns management module can automate parts of the process, such as identifying return reasons, applying restocking fees if applicable, and updating inventory levels accurately.

3. Tracking and Analyzing Return Patterns:

Identifying Common Reasons for Returns: Collecting and analyzing data on returns helps identify patterns, such as sizing issues or product

143

defects. Businesses can use this information to improve product quality or refine descriptions, thus reducing future returns.

Segmentation by Product or Customer Type: Understanding which products or customer demographics are associated with higher return rates can inform decision-making on inventory stocking and return policies.

Impact of Returns on Inventory Levels and Costs

Handling returns effectively is critical because poor reverse logistics can lead to excess inventory, increased handling costs, and diminished profitability. Here's how returns impact inventory and strategies to mitigate associated costs:

1. Inventory Buildup from Returns:

Excess Inventory from Returns: Without an efficient return processing system, companies may accumulate excess stock. This is especially challenging for seasonal or trend-based items, which can lose value quickly if not resold promptly.

Increased Storage Costs: Returned items require storage space, and without prompt processing, they add to storage costs and tie up resources. Over time, this can lead to warehouse inefficiencies and higher operating expenses.

2. Financial Impact of Returns on Margins:

Cost of Processing and Restocking: Returns entail costs for inspection, repackaging, restocking, and in some cases, repair or refurbishment. Restocking fees can offset these costs slightly, but many companies must absorb these additional expenses.

Value Deterioration for Returned Items: Products, especially in fashion or electronics, can depreciate rapidly after purchase. To retain value, businesses should prioritize fast processing and reintroduction of returned items into inventory.

3. Addressing Return-Related Costs Strategically:

Optimizing Return Processing Costs: Outsourcing certain aspects of returns, like inspection and repackaging, or partnering with third-party logistics providers (3PLs) can lower costs and expedite the reverse logistics process.

Reducing Cost Impact Through Dynamic Pricing: Items that are returned and repurposed can be resold at a discount or through secondary channels, maintaining turnover and reducing storage costs while recapturing some value.

Strategies for Repurposing or Reselling Returned Inventory

To mitigate losses associated with returns, businesses can adopt strategies to repurpose or resell items, maximizing reclaimed value. Below are some effective approaches:

1. Refurbishment and Repackaging for Resale:

Repairing and Refurbishing Items: High-value items like electronics or appliances are often repaired or refurbished and then resold at a lower price. Offering refurbished products can attract cost-sensitive customers and maintain sales volume.

Repackaging as 'Open Box' Items: Items returned in good condition with minimal use can be repackaged and sold as "open box" products, typically at a slight discount. This allows companies to recoup most of the item's original value without investing heavily in repairs.

2. Reselling Through Alternative Channels:

Secondary Marketplaces: Selling returned items through secondary marketplaces, such as outlet stores or online discount platforms, enables companies to clear returned inventory without crowding primary sales channels.

Wholesale and Liquidation Sales: For products that may not sell through regular channels, wholesale or liquidation sales offer a way to move returned stock. While these sales yield lower revenue per unit, they help free up warehouse space and reduce holding costs.

3. Donating or Recycling Returns with Low Resale Potential:

Donations for Social Good: Non-profit organizations often accept donated goods, particularly for non-perishable items, offering tax benefits and positive brand exposure.

Recycling or Upcycling: Items with no resale potential can often be recycled or upcycled, especially if they contain valuable materials like metals or plastics. Partnering with recycling firms can help companies dispose of unusable items in an environmentally responsible way, reducing waste and promoting sustainability.

Leveraging Technology in Reverse Logistics and Inventory Reclamation

Technology is essential in streamlining reverse logistics processes, enabling effective return tracking, inventory reclamation, and reprocessing. Here's how technology can support each step:

1. Inventory and Returns Management Systems:

Automated Processing: An advanced WMS can automate receiving, categorizing, and re-stocking returned items. Automated alerts for inspection, categorization, and packaging help speed up returns processing, making it easier to reclaim inventory.

Visibility Across Reverse Logistics Stages: Real-time visibility into returned inventory allows businesses to track items as they move through reverse logistics, improving coordination and minimizing delays.

2. Data Analytics and Return Forecasting:

Predictive Analytics for Return Rates: Analytics tools can forecast return rates based on product categories, customer segments, and seasonal patterns. These insights enable better inventory and cash flow planning.

Root Cause Analysis for Common Return Reasons: Data analytics platforms can help identify root causes of returns, enabling companies to address recurring issues, whether in product design, quality control, or customer experience.

3. IoT and RFID for Enhanced Tracking:

Enhanced Item Tracking: RFID tags and IoT devices provide precise tracking for returned items, improving inventory management efficiency and ensuring returned products are properly categorized and processed.

Quality Control with IoT Sensors: IoT sensors can assess the condition of returned products in transit, such as verifying whether items were damaged during shipping. This ensures that only products in sellable condition are reintegrated into inventory.

4. Automated Returns Processing for Speed and Efficiency:

Automated Inspection and Sorting: Automated systems for inspecting and sorting returns, such as conveyor systems with quality control sensors, can significantly reduce the manual labor required and speed up the process.

Artificial Intelligence for Grading Returned Items: AI-based systems can classify returned items based on their condition, automatically directing them to the appropriate route (resale, refurbishment, or recycling).

Managing reverse logistics and inventory reclamation effectively is essential for companies aiming to minimize costs, optimize inventory, and enhance customer satisfaction. With strategic policies, efficient processing systems, and innovative technology, companies can handle returns effectively, reduce the financial impact of returns, and reclaim value through resale or repurposing. As reverse logistics continue to evolve, businesses that master the complexities of inventory reclamation will be better positioned to remain competitive in a customer-driven marketplace.

Chapter 19: Sustainability in Demand-Driven Inventory Management

Integrating sustainability into demand-driven inventory management is increasingly essential for businesses that aim to reduce their environmental impact while meeting customer expectations. Sustainable inventory practices focus on minimizing waste, reducing excess stock, and optimizing sourcing to meet both environmental goals and demand effectively. This chapter discusses key areas of sustainable inventory management, including setting sustainability goals, minimizing waste, and adopting eco-friendly sourcing practices.

Incorporating Sustainability Goals into Inventory Strategies

For sustainable inventory management, aligning inventory policies with broader corporate sustainability goals is critical. Companies can embed sustainability into inventory planning through objectives like minimizing carbon footprint, prioritizing renewable resources, and reducing emissions associated with storage and transportation.

1. Defining Sustainability Objectives for Inventory:

Environmental Impact Reduction: Goals may include reducing carbon emissions from transportation, minimizing resource consumption, and managing inventory more efficiently to prevent waste.

Tracking Sustainability Metrics: Establishing metrics—such as carbon footprint per SKU, water use, or waste generation—enables companies to monitor the environmental impact of inventory practices and make data-driven decisions to improve sustainability.

2. Aligning Demand Forecasting with Sustainability:

Forecast Accuracy for Waste Reduction: Accurate demand forecasting reduces the risk of overproduction and excess stock, which often leads to waste. Demand-driven forecasting models help avoid surplus inventory, minimizing the need for disposal or heavy discounting.

Sustainable Demand Planning: Incorporating seasonal demand fluctuations, product life cycles, and trends can ensure more precise planning, preventing the environmental impact of producing or transporting unneeded stock.

3. Embedding Sustainability into KPIs and Performance Measures:

Sustainability KPIs: Key Performance Indicators (KPIs) like waste reduction, carbon savings, and resource conservation help assess the effectiveness of sustainable inventory management efforts.

Balanced Scorecards: Using a balanced scorecard approach to combine financial, customer, and sustainability metrics supports a holistic view of performance and sustainability alignment.

Reducing Waste and Excess Inventory

Reducing waste is a foundational aspect of sustainable inventory management, as it directly minimizes environmental impact. Strategies to cut down on inventory waste range from optimizing order quantities to establishing efficient end-of-life product processes.

1. Inventory Optimization and Lean Management:

Lean Inventory Practices: Implementing lean principles, such as Just-In-Time (JIT) inventory, minimizes waste by maintaining only what is needed to meet demand. Reducing buffer stock can help lower costs and environmental impact by preventing overproduction.

Minimizing Overstock and Dead Stock: Data-driven insights can identify slow-moving products and adjust stocking levels, thus reducing waste associated with unsold or expired items. This can also prevent wasteful clearance practices that lead to significant environmental impact.

2. Inventory Reduction through Circular Economy Practices:

Reusing and Recycling: Encouraging reuse or recycling of unsold products minimizes landfill waste. Companies can either reprocess these items for resale or donate them to non-profit organizations.

Return and Repurpose Initiatives: Establishing a reverse logistics system for returns, repairs, or refurbishment contributes to sustainable inventory practices by extending product life cycles.

3. Packaging Optimization for Sustainability:

Reducing Packaging Waste: Using minimal, recyclable, or biodegradable packaging materials reduces environmental impact. Optimizing packaging to use less space in transit also lowers shipping-related emissions.

Eco-Friendly Materials: Replacing traditional packaging with biodegradable or compostable materials can significantly lower the environmental footprint of inventory management processes.

Sustainable Sourcing and Eco-Friendly Inventory Practices

Sustainable sourcing is vital to building an eco-conscious inventory management strategy. By sourcing materials responsibly and prioritizing eco-friendly practices, businesses can support environmental sustainability while aligning with consumer values.

1. Sustainable Procurement Policies:

Ethical and Eco-Friendly Suppliers: Partnering with suppliers who adhere to environmental and ethical standards supports sustainability throughout the supply chain. Companies may prioritize certified suppliers (e.g., Fair Trade, organic, or carbon-neutral) to ensure sustainable sourcing.

Local Sourcing to Reduce Carbon Footprint: Procuring goods locally where feasible minimizes transportation emissions, aligns with sustainable goals, and supports local economies.

2. Prioritizing Renewable and Recycled Materials:

Using Recycled Materials: Incorporating recycled or upcycled materials in product manufacturing helps reduce resource consumption and waste. This is particularly relevant in industries like fashion, electronics, and packaging.

Renewable Resources and Bio-based Materials: Transitioning to renewable resources (e.g., bamboo, hemp) instead of finite resources (e.g., plastic, metal) helps reduce environmental degradation and aligns with sustainable inventory practices.

3. Supplier Collaboration for Sustainable Inventory:

Joint Sustainability Goals: Working closely with suppliers to align sustainability objectives—such as reducing emissions or waste—supports cohesive, environmentally responsible inventory practices.

Vendor-Managed Inventory for Efficiency: Vendor-managed inventory (VMI) can help streamline demand-driven inventory management by reducing stock levels and unnecessary replenishment, resulting in less waste and a smaller environmental footprint.

Sustainability-Driven Demand Forecasting and Planning

Integrating sustainability into demand forecasting ensures that inventory decisions consider both demand patterns and environmental impacts. Sustainability-focused forecasting accounts for the resources required and identifies potential opportunities to reduce excess and minimize waste.

1. Predictive Analytics to Avoid Overproduction:

Demand Analytics for Inventory Optimization: Leveraging predictive analytics for inventory optimization can forecast needs accurately and avoid excess, leading to fewer markdowns and minimized waste.

Scenario Planning for Sustainable Demand Management: Simulating various demand scenarios based on economic or environmental factors allows companies to better plan inventory needs, thus aligning with sustainability objectives.

2. Seasonal Demand Planning with a Sustainability Focus:

Adjusting Inventory for Seasonality: Planning for seasonal demand with sustainability in mind can prevent surplus inventory by aligning stock levels with actual demand, particularly important in industries with seasonal variations like fashion and electronics.

Eco-Friendly Disposal of Excess Inventory: For unavoidable excess, strategies like donating or upcycling unsold stock prevent items from ending up in landfills and support corporate social responsibility goals.

Eco-Friendly Technologies and Innovation in Sustainable Inventory Management

Emerging technologies such as AI, IoT, and blockchain can drive sustainability by optimizing inventory processes and providing real-time visibility. These technologies improve inventory management efficiency and reduce waste.

1. AI for Sustainable Forecasting and Inventory Optimization:

Enhanced Forecasting Accuracy: AI-driven demand forecasting tools help predict demand patterns more accurately, preventing overstock and reducing the environmental impact of unsold products.

Inventory Allocation Optimization: AI algorithms can dynamically allocate inventory across distribution channels based on demand and sustainability criteria, ensuring that products reach consumers with minimal waste.

2. IoT for Real-Time Tracking and Monitoring:

Reducing Waste with IoT Sensors: IoT-enabled sensors provide real-time data on stock levels, product conditions, and warehouse temperatures, enabling better control over perishables or time-sensitive items.

Improving Transportation Efficiency: IoT technology can optimize transportation routes and reduce fuel consumption, thus lowering emissions associated with inventory transportation.

3. Blockchain for Supply Chain Transparency:

Enhanced Visibility and Accountability: Blockchain technology can provide end-to-end transparency, enabling consumers to trace product origins and environmental impact. It fosters accountability and can verify sustainable practices throughout the supply chain.

Reducing Resource Waste: Blockchain facilitates better tracking of materials, minimizing waste by ensuring the right materials are sourced and reducing fraud or duplicate orders.

Sustainability in demand-driven inventory management is about making eco-conscious choices in forecasting, sourcing, and inventory handling. Through sustainable practices such as minimizing waste, optimizing supplier relations, and adopting technology for real-time insights, companies can improve their environmental footprint while meeting demand. In the long term, embedding sustainability into inventory management not only reduces waste and supports eco-friendly practices but also aligns with consumer expectations and strengthens brand reputation in a market increasingly focused on environmental responsibility.

Chapter 20: Inventory Risk Management

Managing inventory effectively involves not only ensuring sufficient stock to meet demand but also preparing for the risks associated with holding inventory. Inventory-related risks can impact profitability, disrupt operations, and ultimately harm a company's reputation. In this chapter, we explore the types of risks associated with inventory, strategies to mitigate these risks, and the importance of contingency planning and recovery strategies to ensure business continuity.

Identifying and Managing Inventory-Related Risks

Inventory-related risks come in various forms, each presenting specific challenges that require proactive management to minimize potential impacts on operations and costs. By understanding the different types of risks, companies can develop targeted strategies to address each risk effectively.

1. Common Types of Inventory Risks:

Obsolescence: Inventory obsolescence occurs when products become outdated or unwanted, often due to shifts in consumer preferences, technological advances, or seasonal demand changes. This can lead to costly markdowns or write-offs if the stock cannot be sold.

Shrinkage: Shrinkage is the loss of inventory due to theft, damage, administrative errors, or fraud. It affects physical inventory counts and reduces the value of available stock, often resulting in a direct hit to the bottom line.

Stockouts: A stockout occurs when inventory runs out before replenishment, leading to missed sales opportunities, frustrated customers, and potential harm to brand loyalty.

Demand Variability: Unpredictable changes in customer demand can create overstock or understock situations, leading to either higher holding costs or stockouts.

Quality Defects: Poor-quality inventory can lead to returns, recalls, or damage to brand reputation, especially in cases where defective products reach customers.

2. Techniques for Identifying Inventory Risks:

Inventory Audits: Regular inventory audits help identify discrepancies between recorded and actual inventory, allowing companies to spot trends in shrinkage, obsolescence, and demand changes.

Risk Assessment Tools: Tools such as risk matrices or failure mode and effects analysis (FMEA) can help assess the likelihood and potential impact of various risks, allowing managers to prioritize the most critical risks.

Data Analytics: By analyzing past inventory and sales data, companies can predict patterns that might indicate potential risks, such as seasonal demand shifts, slow-moving stock, or high return rates.

Mitigating Risks Such as Obsolescence, Shrinkage, and Stockouts

Once identified, inventory risks can be mitigated through a combination of strategic policies, technology, and operational controls. Below are specific approaches to manage the risks of obsolescence, shrinkage, and stockouts.

1. Mitigating Obsolescence Risks:

Demand Forecasting: Accurate demand forecasting reduces the likelihood of overstocking items with limited shelf life or fluctuating demand. Incorporating seasonal and market trends into forecasts can improve accuracy.

Inventory Turnover Optimization: Keeping inventory turnover high helps minimize the chances of products becoming obsolete. Strategies like Just-In-Time (JIT) inventory and agile ordering allow companies to align stock levels more closely with current demand.

Product Lifecycle Management: For items with known lifespans, like electronics or fashion, it's critical to plan for end-of-life transitions by gradually reducing order quantities and offering discounts to sell through inventory before obsolescence.

2. Managing Shrinkage:

Enhanced Security Measures: Shrinkage due to theft can be reduced through physical security measures, such as surveillance cameras, access controls, and regular stock inspections.

Inventory Tracking Systems: Technologies like RFID, barcoding, and automated inventory systems can help track stock in real time, reducing human errors, deterring theft, and enabling swift corrective actions when discrepancies arise.

Employee Training and Policies: Educating employees on best practices for inventory handling, record-keeping, and theft prevention can lower the risk of accidental shrinkage and internal theft.

3. Preventing Stockouts:

Safety Stock: Maintaining a buffer of safety stock is a common way to guard against demand fluctuations, supplier delays, and lead time variability. Safety stock levels should be carefully calibrated based on demand patterns and supplier reliability.

Reorder Point Systems: Establishing reorder points based on lead times and demand forecasts can ensure timely replenishment before stockouts occur. Continuous review systems, where stock levels are monitored in real-time, are particularly effective for high-demand items.

Supplier Reliability and Collaboration: Reliable suppliers reduce the risk of delays or product shortages. Building strong partnerships, using dual sourcing, and incorporating vendor-managed inventory (VMI) can further minimize stockouts.

Contingency Planning and Inventory Recovery Strategies

A robust contingency plan ensures that inventory management is resilient to unexpected disruptions. From natural disasters to supply chain disruptions, having well-defined recovery strategies can help minimize the impact of adverse events on inventory levels and overall operations.

1. Developing an Effective Contingency Plan:

Risk Assessment and Scenario Planning: Companies should identify high-impact risks and create action plans to address scenarios such as supplier failure, transportation delays, and demand surges. Scenario planning enables companies to test various response strategies in a controlled environment.

Backup Suppliers and Dual Sourcing: Relying on a single supplier for critical items is risky. Dual sourcing or maintaining backup suppliers ensures that if one source becomes unavailable, alternative options are already in place to prevent stockouts.

Inventory Buffering Strategies: For essential products, maintaining additional stock or "strategic reserves" can provide a cushion during supply chain disruptions. Inventory buffering can be location-specific, depending on the vulnerability of certain areas to risks like natural disasters.

2. Inventory Recovery Strategies Post-Disruption:

Quick Response Replenishment: In the event of a stockout or disaster, quick response replenishment strategies, such as expediting orders or increasing production, can help restore inventory levels quickly.

Flexible Distribution Networks: Having flexible warehousing and distribution networks allows for inventory to be reallocated as needed. For example, if one distribution center is affected, inventory can be redirected from another location to meet demand.

Customer Communication and Transparency: In cases where stockouts are unavoidable, clear and transparent communication with customers can help mitigate negative impacts on brand loyalty. Offering pre-orders, providing realistic lead times, or suggesting alternative products can keep customer satisfaction intact.

3. Leveraging Technology for Resilient Inventory Management:

Real-Time Inventory Monitoring: IoT sensors, RFID technology, and inventory management software enable real-time monitoring of stock levels, helping companies to respond immediately to sudden changes in inventory status.

Predictive Analytics and AI: Using predictive analytics to anticipate potential disruptions based on data trends can improve inventory planning and readiness. AI algorithms can assist in assessing supplier reliability, predicting demand surges, and even recommending optimal stock levels based on changing conditions.

Blockchain for Supply Chain Transparency: Blockchain provides an immutable record of transactions, making it easier to track and verify the movement of inventory across the supply chain. This transparency helps ensure accountability, supports collaboration with suppliers, and reduces fraud risks.

Balancing Cost and Risk in Inventory Management

Achieving an optimal balance between minimizing risks and controlling costs is a central challenge in inventory management. While higher stock levels can mitigate the risk of stockouts, they also increase holding costs and the risk of obsolescence.

1. Cost-Benefit Analysis for Inventory Risk Management:

Evaluating Risk vs. Holding Cost: Inventory managers must weigh the benefits of holding safety stock against the associated carrying costs, including storage, insurance, and potential obsolescence.

Dynamic Inventory Policies: In demand-driven inventory management, policies should adapt to shifting risk profiles. For example, during peak seasons, companies might increase safety stock levels to meet demand, while reducing it during off-peak periods to minimize costs.

2. Inventory Management Software for Balancing Risk and Cost:

Automated Decision-Making: Inventory management software can automate reorder points, safety stock levels, and even order quantities based on real-time demand data, reducing the burden on managers and improving efficiency.

Optimization Models: Advanced optimization models, like Economic Order Quantity (EOQ) and Multi-Echelon Inventory Optimization (MEIO), can help determine the best balance between service levels and inventory costs by factoring in demand, lead time, and risk tolerance.

Inventory risk management is essential for companies that want to maintain resilience and efficiency while managing inventory. By identifying common risks such as obsolescence, shrinkage, and stockouts, and implementing strategies to mitigate these risks, companies can minimize disruptions and protect profitability. Additionally, contingency planning and inventory recovery strategies ensure that companies are prepared for unexpected events, while technology and real-time monitoring enable a proactive approach to inventory risk management. Ultimately, a balance between risk and cost is key to maintaining an effective inventory system that supports business goals and customer satisfaction.

Chapter 21: Cost Management in Demand-Driven Inventory

Effective cost management is essential for demand-driven inventory systems, where meeting customer demand is balanced against the costs of holding and managing inventory. This chapter delves into the key types of inventory costs, strategies for controlling these costs, and the challenge of balancing cost efficiency with service level goals.

Breakdown of Inventory Costs

Inventory costs are generally categorized into holding, ordering, and stockout costs. Each cost type has a distinct impact on a company's bottom line and requires tailored strategies for effective management.

1. Holding Costs:

Holding costs, also known as carrying costs, are incurred from storing unsold inventory. This category includes:

Storage and Warehousing Costs: Rent, utilities, and depreciation of storage facilities.

Insurance and Security: Costs for insuring inventory and securing the warehouse.

Capital Costs: The opportunity cost of capital tied up in inventory, which could otherwise be invested.

Obsolescence and Depreciation: The risk of inventory losing value over time, especially for items with a limited shelf life.

Holding costs often represent a significant portion of total inventory costs, making it essential to optimize stock levels without compromising service.

2. Ordering Costs:

Ordering costs are associated with the process of replenishing inventory, including:

166

Administrative Expenses: Time and resources spent on placing and managing orders.

Transportation Costs: Costs for shipping inventory, whether inbound from suppliers or outbound to other locations.

Handling and Inspection: Labor and resources needed to receive, inspect, and store incoming inventory.

Ordering costs can be managed by optimizing order frequencies and batch sizes, often using models like Economic Order Quantity (EOQ).

3. Stockout Costs:

Stockout costs arise when inventory levels are insufficient to meet customer demand. These costs can be challenging to quantify but are crucial to consider as they affect both revenue and customer satisfaction. Stockout costs include:

Lost Sales and Revenue: Missed opportunities when customers turn to competitors.

Customer Dissatisfaction and Loyalty Impact: Unfulfilled orders can harm brand reputation and customer loyalty.

Backorder Management: Costs for handling backorders, expedited shipping, and labor needed to address the issue.

Preventing stockouts often requires maintaining safety stock and buffer inventory, though these measures increase holding costs.

Cost Control Strategies in Demand-Driven Inventory

In demand-driven inventory systems, cost control strategies aim to reduce excess costs while maintaining the agility to meet dynamic

167

customer demands. Below are some effective strategies for managing inventory-related expenses.

1. Batch Sizes and Order Frequency Optimization:

Economic Order Quantity (EOQ): EOQ is a formula that helps companies find the ideal order quantity to minimize total ordering and holding costs. This model considers demand rate, order cost, and holding cost.

Vendor-Managed Inventory (VMI): With VMI, suppliers monitor and manage inventory levels, often reducing ordering costs and potentially optimizing batch sizes.

Just-in-Time (JIT): JIT minimizes holding costs by reducing inventory levels and receiving products only as needed. However, it requires reliable suppliers and can be vulnerable to supply chain disruptions.

2. Supplier Terms and Agreements:

Negotiated Payment Terms: Favorable payment terms, such as extended credit periods, can reduce capital costs by delaying cash outflows.

Volume Discounts and Incentives: Negotiating for bulk discounts or loyalty incentives can lower per-unit ordering costs, though care should be taken to avoid overstocking.

Collaborative Planning, Forecasting, and Replenishment (CPFR): Collaborating with suppliers on demand forecasting and inventory replenishment can reduce costs related to over-ordering or frequent reordering.

3. Inventory Turnover Improvement:

Cycle Counting: Regularly reviewing stock levels and adjusting replenishment practices can prevent excess holding costs and stockouts.

ABC Analysis: ABC analysis categorizes inventory by value and usage frequency, enabling focused control over high-value items while optimizing less critical stock.

Dynamic Stock Levels: Adjusting stock levels based on seasonal demand and historical sales data can reduce overstocking during slow periods while ensuring readiness for peak seasons.

4. Minimizing Stockout Costs with Safety Stock:

Safety Stock Calculation: Using statistical models to calculate optimal safety stock levels based on demand variability and lead time can prevent costly stockouts.

Demand Forecasting and Demand Sensing: By using real-time data and predictive analytics, companies can improve forecast accuracy, reducing the likelihood of unexpected demand surges that lead to stockouts.

Flexible Fulfillment Options: Employing multiple fulfillment centers or dropshipping partners can help companies respond quickly to demand spikes without maintaining excessive inventory.

5. Reducing Waste and Obsolescence:

First-In, First-Out (FIFO) System: This method ensures that older inventory is sold or used first, which is particularly useful for perishable or time-sensitive products.

Markdown and Clearance Strategies: Offering discounts on slow-moving stock can reduce holding costs and free up space for high-demand items.

Inventory Audits and Monitoring: Frequent audits help identify obsolete or low-turnover stock, enabling managers to act quickly to prevent excess holding costs.

Balancing Cost Efficiency with Service Level Goals

Maintaining a balance between inventory costs and customer service levels is essential for demand-driven inventory management. While cost efficiency is critical, it should not come at the expense of customer satisfaction.

1. Service Level Goals:

Service levels define the degree to which a company meets customer demand without stockouts. Higher service levels generally require higher safety stock levels, which increases holding costs. Therefore, companies must set realistic service level goals that align with customer expectations and business objectives.

2. Trade-Off Analysis:

A trade-off analysis evaluates the cost-benefit relationship between service levels and inventory costs. For instance, a higher safety stock might improve service levels but increase holding costs. Companies can use metrics like fill rate, on-time delivery, and customer satisfaction to gauge service levels and find a balanced approach.

3. Customer Segmentation and Inventory Strategies:

Segmentation Based on Demand Patterns: Segmenting customers or products by demand variability allows companies to apply tailored inventory strategies. For instance, high-demand items may have higher safety stock, while low-demand items are kept at minimal levels.

Differentiated Service Levels: Not all products require the same service level. Companies can set lower service levels for less critical products to reduce costs while maintaining high service levels for key items.

4. Continuous Improvement in Cost Management:

Inventory cost management is not a one-time activity. Regular assessments and adjustments help companies adapt to changing market conditions and demand patterns.

Lean Inventory Practices: Lean practices such as eliminating waste, reducing lead times, and optimizing workflows improve inventory cost efficiency.

Kaizen and Six Sigma Techniques: Continuous improvement techniques, such as Kaizen and Six Sigma, can help identify and eliminate cost inefficiencies across inventory processes.

Performance Metrics and KPIs: Tracking key performance indicators (KPIs) like inventory turnover, carrying cost percentage, and stockout frequency provides insights into cost management effectiveness.

5. Advanced Technology for Cost Management:

Inventory Management Software: Automated systems enable real-time tracking of stock levels, reorder points, and lead times, helping managers make informed cost-saving decisions.

Predictive Analytics and Machine Learning: By forecasting demand trends and identifying patterns in cost data, predictive analytics can optimize order quantities and minimize stockouts.

Supply Chain Visibility Tools: End-to-end visibility helps companies control costs by improving coordination with suppliers, predicting disruptions, and responding proactively.

Cost management in demand-driven inventory is a balancing act that requires strategic approaches to minimize holding, ordering, and stockout costs while ensuring high service levels. Effective cost management involves understanding the types of inventory costs, employing targeted cost control strategies, and continually evaluating performance to align costs with business objectives and customer expectations. By leveraging technology, optimizing order sizes, and collaborating with suppliers, companies can reduce inventory costs and improve the efficiency of their demand-driven inventory systems. The ultimate goal is to maintain a resilient inventory strategy that is both cost-effective and capable of meeting dynamic customer demands.

Chapter 22: Continuous Improvement in Inventory Management

In demand-driven inventory management, maintaining efficiency and reducing waste require a commitment to continuous improvement. This chapter focuses on applying Lean and Six Sigma principles to inventory processes, the role of Kaizen in fostering a culture of ongoing enhancement, and setting effective metrics and KPIs to track and measure progress.

Applying Lean and Six Sigma to Inventory Processes

Lean and Six Sigma methodologies are powerful tools for improving inventory management by eliminating waste and enhancing efficiency.

1. Lean Inventory Management:

Lean principles aim to reduce non-value-added activities, streamline processes, and improve overall efficiency. In inventory management, this translates to:

Minimizing Excess Inventory: Avoiding overstocking, which ties up capital and increases holding costs.

Reducing Lead Times: Streamlining workflows to ensure that products are available when needed without excessive buffer stock.

Eliminating Wastes in Handling and Storage: Lean techniques like the 5S (Sort, Set in Order, Shine, Standardize, Sustain) method organize inventory spaces for better accessibility and reduce unnecessary movement.

2. Six Sigma in Inventory Management:

Six Sigma focuses on minimizing variability and achieving high-quality outcomes. Key Six Sigma tools for inventory management include:

DMAIC (Define, Measure, Analyze, Improve, Control): This structured methodology is used to improve processes by identifying and addressing root causes of inefficiencies in inventory.

Root Cause Analysis (RCA): Techniques such as the Fishbone Diagram and 5 Whys identify underlying issues that lead to excess inventory, stockouts, or delays.

Process Capability Analysis: This analysis measures how well inventory processes meet customer demand and expectations, guiding improvements to enhance service levels.

3. Lean Six Sigma Integration:

Combining Lean and Six Sigma methodologies enables organizations to benefit from Lean's focus on waste reduction and Six Sigma's emphasis on quality and precision. Together, these approaches help inventory managers:

Reduce order cycle times and enhance accuracy in demand forecasts.

Improve stock accuracy and reduce costs associated with mismanaged inventory.

Ensure processes are aligned with the organization's demand-driven approach.

Kaizen and Continuous Improvement for Inventory Efficiency

Kaizen, meaning "change for better" in Japanese, is a continuous improvement philosophy that encourages incremental changes, empowering employees to improve processes regularly.

1. Implementing Kaizen in Inventory Management:

Kaizen principles emphasize that small, ongoing improvements can accumulate to create significant efficiencies. In inventory management, Kaizen initiatives may involve:

Daily or Weekly Improvement Routines: Encouraging employees to identify and act on small changes that improve workflow and reduce waste.

Employee Involvement: Engaging warehouse staff, inventory managers, and procurement teams in problem-solving can reveal insights from those directly involved in the inventory process.

Kaizen Events: Focused, short-term projects address specific inventory challenges, such as reducing stockout rates or improving picking accuracy.

2. Tools for Continuous Improvement under Kaizen:

Several tools support Kaizen-based continuous improvement, including:

Standard Work: Documenting the best-known process for each inventory task creates a baseline that can be reviewed and improved over time.

Value Stream Mapping: Mapping the flow of materials and information helps identify bottlenecks and opportunities to optimize inventory processes.

Gemba Walks: By observing inventory operations firsthand, managers and leaders can identify inefficiencies and areas for improvement directly within the workspace.

3. Creating a Culture of Continuous Improvement:

Fostering a culture of continuous improvement requires more than tools; it requires commitment across all levels of the organization. This can be achieved by:

Encouraging Open Communication: Employees should feel comfortable suggesting improvements and highlighting challenges without fear of reprimand.

Rewarding Improvement Initiatives: Recognizing and rewarding contributions to process improvements helps motivate employees to actively participate in ongoing enhancement.

Training and Development: Providing Lean and Six Sigma training for staff enhances their ability to contribute effectively to continuous improvement.

Setting Metrics and KPIs for Ongoing Improvement

Measuring progress in continuous improvement is essential to ensure that changes lead to meaningful outcomes. Setting the right metrics and key performance indicators (KPIs) provides visibility into inventory management performance and highlights areas that require attention.

1. Key Inventory KPIs for Continuous Improvement:

Inventory Turnover Ratio: This metric indicates how often inventory is sold and replaced over a period. Higher turnover rates suggest effective inventory management, while lower rates indicate potential overstocking.

Days Inventory Outstanding (DIO): DIO measures the average number of days inventory is held before it's sold. Lower DIO can mean more efficient inventory management, reducing holding costs.

Fill Rate: The percentage of customer orders that are filled on the first shipment. A high fill rate reflects better inventory availability and customer satisfaction.

Stockout Rate: Tracking the frequency of stockouts helps identify issues in demand forecasting or replenishment, guiding improvements to reduce lost sales.

Order Cycle Time: The time it takes to fulfill a customer order. Reducing order cycle time enhances customer satisfaction and supports a lean inventory system.

Carrying Cost of Inventory: This KPI tracks the total cost of holding inventory, including storage, insurance, and capital costs. Monitoring this helps keep holding costs in check and encourages efficient stock management.

2. Setting Improvement Targets:

Establishing targets for each KPI is crucial for driving continuous improvement. Targets should be:

SMART (Specific, Measurable, Achievable, Relevant, Time-Bound): Clear targets enable teams to understand what they're working toward and provide a timeline for achieving improvements.

Aligned with Business Goals: Inventory KPIs should support broader objectives, such as cost reduction, service level improvements, or enhanced agility.

Reviewed Regularly: Regular review of targets ensures they remain relevant to changing demand patterns or business priorities.

3. Monitoring and Adapting Improvement Efforts:

Continuous improvement requires ongoing evaluation. Regularly reviewing performance against KPIs allows companies to identify trends and adjust improvement strategies as needed. Tools for monitoring include:

Dashboards and Reports: Inventory management software often includes dashboards to track real-time performance on key metrics.

Root Cause Analysis for Deviations: When KPIs show underperformance, root cause analysis can pinpoint the underlying issues, whether they stem from supplier delays, demand fluctuations, or process inefficiencies.

Benchmarking: Comparing inventory performance against industry benchmarks helps set realistic targets and understand how the organization's performance aligns with peers.

Continuous improvement in inventory management is a proactive approach to meeting demand while maintaining efficiency and reducing waste. By applying Lean and Six Sigma, organizations can streamline processes, cut unnecessary costs, and increase accuracy in inventory control. Kaizen further enhances efficiency by encouraging incremental, everyday improvements that accumulate over time, creating a culture of ongoing enhancement.

Setting meaningful metrics and KPIs ensures that progress is measurable and provides insight into areas requiring attention. By maintaining a focus on continuous improvement, companies can adapt to changes in demand and the supply chain landscape, ensuring inventory management practices remain agile and responsive. Through dedication to these principles, organizations can realize long-term benefits, improve customer satisfaction, and gain a competitive edge in the market.

Chapter 23: Case Studies in Demand-Driven Inventory

In demand-driven inventory management, real-world examples illustrate the benefits of aligning inventory with demand patterns to improve service levels, reduce costs, and enhance efficiency. This chapter delves into notable case studies across various industries—retail, manufacturing, and healthcare—to explore how organizations have successfully implemented demand-driven inventory practices. Each example offers unique insights and valuable lessons applicable to businesses of all sizes and sectors.

Real-World Examples of Successful Demand-Driven Inventory Practices

Implementing demand-driven inventory practices requires strategic planning, the right technology, and often, cultural change. Here, we explore a few organizations that have achieved significant success with demand-driven inventory models.

1. Walmart: Leveraging Data for Inventory Efficiency in Retail

As a leader in demand-driven inventory management, Walmart uses real-time data analytics and sophisticated technology to anticipate demand and adjust inventory levels accordingly. With an extensive network of suppliers and distribution centers, Walmart integrates point-of-sale (POS) data, supply chain analytics, and demand forecasting tools to ensure that stores are stocked with the right products at the right time.

Key Strategies: Walmart uses a vendor-managed inventory (VMI) approach, allowing suppliers to monitor inventory levels and replenish stock as needed. This collaboration enhances transparency and reduces stockouts.

Outcome: By accurately forecasting demand, Walmart minimizes excess inventory and reduces costs, achieving a high level of customer satisfaction.

Takeaway: Collaborative inventory management and data-driven forecasting can enable retailers to synchronize supply with demand effectively.

2. Toyota: Demand-Driven Inventory in Manufacturing

Toyota's Just-in-Time (JIT) system exemplifies demand-driven inventory management in manufacturing. By only producing what is needed to meet immediate demand, Toyota minimizes inventory holding costs and enhances production flexibility.

Key Strategies: Toyota uses kanban cards to signal when parts need to be replenished, aligning production closely with demand. This pull-based approach limits excess inventory and reduces waste.

Outcome: The JIT model allows Toyota to maintain lean operations, improve quality, and adapt quickly to market changes.

Takeaway: A pull-based system can reduce inventory waste and enhance operational efficiency, but it requires robust supplier relationships to respond swiftly to demand changes.

3. Amazon: Adapting to Demand Fluctuations in E-commerce

Amazon's demand-driven inventory approach is tailored to the fast-paced e-commerce environment, where demand can shift rapidly. Through advanced algorithms and machine learning, Amazon can forecast demand patterns, manage seasonal surges, and optimize stock levels across its extensive fulfillment network.

Key Strategies: Amazon employs predictive analytics to manage inventory, taking into account factors like browsing behavior, historical demand, and external trends. During peak periods, such as the holiday season, Amazon adjusts inventory policies and stocking levels to ensure availability.

Outcome: This adaptive model enables Amazon to fulfill customer orders quickly while minimizing the risk of overstocking.

Takeaway: Predictive analytics can help e-commerce companies respond dynamically to changing demand, enabling efficient, customer-focused inventory management.

Lessons from Various Industries: Retail, Manufacturing, and Healthcare

Demand-driven inventory practices differ across industries, with each sector facing unique challenges and opportunities.

1. Retail: Zara's Agile Inventory Approach

Fast-fashion retailer Zara uses a demand-driven model to stay responsive to the latest fashion trends and customer demand. Rather than relying on long production cycles, Zara designs, manufactures, and delivers new clothing lines to stores in a matter of weeks.

Key Strategies: Zara leverages a demand-driven approach by maintaining short product life cycles, using small production batches, and restocking based on customer demand in each store. Data from store sales directly informs inventory replenishment decisions, reducing excess stock.

Outcome: Zara's model allows it to keep inventory levels low while offering fresh merchandise, enhancing customer satisfaction and brand loyalty.

Takeaway: Flexibility and rapid response to demand can create a competitive edge in industries where trends shift quickly.

2. Healthcare: Mayo Clinic's Approach to Demand-Driven Inventory for Critical Supplies

In the healthcare sector, maintaining inventory for critical medical supplies without incurring unnecessary holding costs is crucial. Mayo Clinic's demand-driven inventory model ensures a balance between availability and efficiency, particularly for high-demand items like personal protective equipment (PPE) and medical devices.

Key Strategies: Mayo Clinic utilizes real-time inventory tracking and demand forecasting for essential supplies. Automated ordering systems help maintain optimal stock levels, ensuring quick replenishment without excessive stockpiling.

Outcome: The demand-driven model ensures that essential supplies are available when needed, improving patient care while keeping costs manageable.

Takeaway: In healthcare, demand-driven inventory management can save lives by ensuring critical supplies are available, highlighting the importance of real-time tracking and automated replenishment.

3. Automotive: General Motors' Shift to Demand-Driven Production

General Motors (GM) adopted a demand-driven approach by implementing a flexible manufacturing strategy, allowing it to produce vehicles based on real-time customer demand. With fluctuating demand patterns, especially during global disruptions, GM moved to a model that aligns production more closely with consumer preferences.

Key Strategies: GM uses predictive analytics and modular manufacturing techniques to adjust production lines quickly based on demand forecasts. This approach minimizes inventory holding costs and increases agility.

Outcome: GM's demand-driven inventory model reduces overproduction and allows the company to respond rapidly to changes in consumer demand.

Takeaway: In industries with long lead times, such as automotive manufacturing, a flexible production approach aligned with real-time demand can mitigate risks associated with excess inventory.

Key Takeaways from Demand-Driven Transformations

Analyzing these examples reveals several common themes and lessons in demand-driven inventory management:

1. The Power of Data and Technology

Data-driven insights and advanced technologies, such as machine learning and real-time tracking, are fundamental to successful demand-driven inventory management. They enable organizations to forecast demand accurately, streamline replenishment, and maintain optimal inventory levels.

2. Importance of Collaboration

Many successful demand-driven inventory models involve collaboration with suppliers and stakeholders. Strong supplier relationships, as seen in Walmart and Toyota's approaches, facilitate timely replenishment, reduce lead times, and improve overall supply chain resilience.

3. Flexibility and Responsiveness

Companies like Amazon and Zara demonstrate the value of flexibility and responsiveness in adapting to demand fluctuations. By shortening production cycles and using pull-based systems, these companies can adapt quickly to changes in demand, minimize excess inventory, and stay competitive.

4. Sector-Specific Considerations

While the demand-driven approach is valuable across industries, each sector must adapt it to its specific needs. For instance, healthcare focuses on critical supply availability, while e-commerce emphasizes quick fulfillment for customer satisfaction. Recognizing industry-specific demands allows companies to tailor demand-driven practices effectively.

5. Continuous Improvement

Demand-driven inventory management is an ongoing process. Organizations that adopt continuous improvement practices, such as Lean and Six Sigma, can refine their inventory models to stay aligned with changing market conditions and customer expectations.

Case studies from various sectors highlight how demand-driven inventory management enhances efficiency, reduces costs, and improves customer satisfaction. These examples demonstrate that aligning inventory with demand patterns requires data, collaboration, flexibility, and industry-specific adaptations. By understanding and applying the lessons from these real-world transformations, organizations can create a demand-driven inventory strategy that meets their unique needs, enabling them to thrive in today's competitive market.

This case study exploration reinforces that demand-driven inventory management is a powerful strategy with broad applicability. Whether in retail, healthcare, or manufacturing, businesses can gain significant benefits by committing to demand-aligned processes and continuous improvement.

Chapter 24: Future Trends in Demand-Driven Inventory

The future of demand-driven inventory management is evolving at a rapid pace, thanks to advancements in artificial intelligence (AI), machine learning, and predictive analytics. Emerging technologies like autonomous inventory systems and real-time data integration are pushing the boundaries of what's possible in inventory management, offering new ways to optimize stock levels, anticipate demand fluctuations, and streamline supply chains. However, with these advancements come unique challenges and opportunities that will shape how companies approach inventory management in the years to come.

Impact of AI, Machine Learning, and Advanced Analytics

AI and machine learning are transforming demand-driven inventory management, offering sophisticated tools to process large amounts of data, make predictions, and automate decision-making processes. These technologies enable companies to align inventory levels with dynamic demand patterns more accurately, effectively bridging the gap between supply and demand.

1. Enhanced Demand Forecasting

Traditional forecasting methods are limited by their reliance on historical data, which may not fully capture complex, evolving demand patterns. AI and machine learning algorithms, however, can analyze both historical and real-time data from diverse sources (e.g., social media trends, economic indicators, and weather patterns), offering a much more granular demand forecast.

Example: Retailers use AI to predict demand spikes based on external factors, like weather forecasts or regional events, enabling better stock management ahead of anticipated demand changes.

2. Predictive Analytics for Proactive Inventory Management

Predictive analytics allows companies to anticipate potential stockouts or overstock situations by identifying patterns and trends in demand data. This foresight enables more proactive management, as companies can respond to anticipated needs rather than reacting to shortages or excess inventory after they occur.

Example: In the automotive industry, predictive analytics can help anticipate parts shortages and adjust stock levels accordingly, especially in response to global supply chain disruptions.

3. Automation in Inventory Replenishment

AI-driven inventory systems can automate replenishment decisions by continuously monitoring stock levels and ordering products only when needed. By integrating with real-time data sources, these systems can maintain optimal inventory levels without human intervention.

Example: Large e-commerce companies use AI to automatically reorder popular products, ensuring they are always in stock and reducing the risk of backorders.

Autonomous Inventory Management and Predictive Technologies

Autonomous inventory management systems are reshaping how organizations handle stock, from the factory floor to warehouses and distribution centers. These technologies use robotics, the Internet of Things (IoT), and other advanced systems to streamline and automate inventory tasks, providing both accuracy and efficiency that were previously unattainable.

1. Robotics and Automated Warehousing

The use of robots in inventory management is becoming increasingly common. Autonomous robots can handle tasks like picking, packing, and transporting items within warehouses, improving both speed and accuracy while reducing labor costs.

Example: Amazon's fulfillment centers utilize robotics for inventory picking, which allows them to process high volumes of orders quickly and accurately, particularly during peak shopping periods.

2. IoT for Real-Time Inventory Monitoring

IoT technology enables real-time tracking of inventory across the supply chain. IoT sensors and devices collect data on inventory levels, location, and condition, feeding this information into centralized management systems. This visibility allows companies to make informed decisions and respond to issues like delayed shipments or temperature-sensitive goods.

Example: Cold chain logistics companies use IoT to monitor the temperature of perishable goods in transit, ensuring that the inventory arrives in optimal condition and reducing waste.

3. Predictive Maintenance for Inventory Optimization

Predictive maintenance, powered by IoT and machine learning, allows companies to monitor the condition of their equipment and anticipate maintenance needs. In industries with complex machinery (e.g., manufacturing), this reduces the likelihood of unplanned downtime, ensuring that production remains steady and demand is met without delays.

Example: A manufacturing company using predictive maintenance can minimize disruptions by scheduling repairs during low-demand periods, maintaining a consistent flow of goods without impacting inventory levels.

Future Challenges and Opportunities for Demand-Driven Inventory

While advanced technologies present exciting opportunities, there are also challenges that companies must address as they move toward demand-driven inventory systems.

1. Data Integration and Security

As companies adopt more technology-driven inventory systems, they must integrate data from multiple sources and ensure it flows seamlessly across the organization. However, the integration of data from various platforms can be challenging, particularly when dealing with legacy systems. Additionally, securing sensitive information against cyber threats becomes more complex as data systems become interconnected.

Opportunity: Cloud-based systems and blockchain technology can enhance data integration and security, offering decentralized, tamper-resistant solutions for sharing inventory data across the supply chain.

2. Skilled Workforce and Change Management

The adoption of AI, robotics, and IoT in inventory management requires a skilled workforce capable of managing and maintaining these technologies. Companies must also address change management as employees adapt to a demand-driven model that increasingly relies on automation and advanced analytics.

Opportunity: Investing in training and development programs can help employees adapt to new technologies, creating a more tech-savvy workforce equipped to handle future innovations.

3. Adapting to Demand Fluctuations and External Shocks

Demand-driven inventory management relies on accurate demand forecasts, but unpredictable events—like pandemics, natural disasters, or economic crises—can disrupt even the most sophisticated models. Companies must prepare for these uncertainties by building resilience and flexibility into their inventory strategies.

Opportunity: Demand-driven inventory management can benefit from scenario planning and contingency buffers, which can help organizations respond quickly to demand fluctuations or unexpected disruptions.

4. Environmental and Regulatory Considerations

As sustainability becomes increasingly important, companies are under pressure to reduce waste and carbon emissions in their inventory practices. Regulations around sustainability, especially in regions with stringent environmental policies, will continue to shape inventory management strategies.

Opportunity: Using AI to optimize delivery routes and reduce waste, as well as sourcing eco-friendly materials, can help companies meet regulatory demands and improve their sustainability efforts.

Conclusion

The future of demand-driven inventory management lies at the intersection of advanced technology, data analytics, and evolving supply chain strategies. AI, machine learning, and IoT will continue to drive inventory optimization, transforming how companies predict, plan, and manage their stock. As autonomous systems become more prevalent, organizations will be able to respond to demand fluctuations in real-time, minimizing costs and enhancing customer satisfaction.

However, the journey toward a fully autonomous, demand-driven inventory model will require overcoming challenges related to data integration, workforce adaptation, and external uncertainties. Companies that can successfully navigate these challenges will be well-positioned to harness the power of demand-driven inventory management, leveraging technology not just for operational efficiency but as a strategic asset in a rapidly evolving marketplace.

By staying informed of future trends and proactively adopting innovative practices, companies can ensure their demand-driven inventory models are resilient, sustainable, and responsive to the demands of tomorrow.

Chapter 25: Conclusion: Building a Demand-Driven Inventory Culture

As businesses transition to demand-driven inventory management, the foundation of long-term success lies in creating an organizational culture that supports and nurtures these principles. Demand-driven inventory management is not solely about implementing the right tools and processes; it requires a comprehensive mindset shift across the organization, from leadership to operational teams. This chapter delves into the steps organizations must take to establish a demand-driven culture, invest in training and development, and lay the groundwork for sustained success in today's dynamic and competitive market environment.

Integrating Demand-Driven Principles into Organizational Culture

Transitioning to a demand-driven inventory approach requires aligning organizational goals, behaviors, and values with the principles that underlie this methodology. When an organization embraces a demand-driven approach, it adopts a mindset that prioritizes customer needs, agile responses, and real-time data-driven decision-making. Integrating these principles into the company culture ensures that demand-driven practices are upheld in day-to-day operations and long-term strategic decisions.

1. Emphasizing Customer-Centricity

In demand-driven inventory management, customer demand and satisfaction are central. This customer-centric approach must permeate the organization's culture, encouraging teams to prioritize customers' needs in inventory-related decisions, service levels, and response times.

Actionable Step: Incorporate customer-focused metrics, like service level and on-time delivery rates, into performance evaluations and key

194

performance indicators (KPIs) for all inventory management and supply chain roles.

2. Encouraging Data-Driven Decision-Making

Demand-driven inventory management relies on real-time data to make decisions. Instilling a data-driven mindset ensures that teams value and utilize accurate, timely data when managing inventory, forecasting demand, and adjusting stock levels.

Actionable Step: Invest in training employees on how to interpret data analytics reports and encourage data transparency across departments to support informed, aligned decision-making.

3. Fostering Collaboration Across Departments

Successful demand-driven inventory management involves close collaboration among departments such as procurement, sales, marketing, and finance. Cross-functional alignment helps ensure that inventory strategies align with organizational goals and market dynamics.

Actionable Step: Hold regular interdepartmental meetings to discuss inventory status, upcoming promotions, and anticipated changes in demand. Establish shared goals across departments to drive cohesion.

Training and Developing Inventory Management Teams

The transition to demand-driven inventory management also hinges on skilled, knowledgeable teams capable of adapting to new methodologies and technologies. Continuous training and development are crucial for empowering staff to effectively execute demand-driven strategies, utilize technological tools, and respond to market changes.

1. Providing Comprehensive Training on Demand-Driven Methodologies

As companies move to a demand-driven approach, it's essential that employees at all levels are well-versed in its core principles, such as real-time demand tracking, dynamic replenishment, and customer-first thinking.

Actionable Step: Develop a structured training program covering demand-driven inventory fundamentals, including demand sensing, demand shaping, and DDMRP (Demand-Driven MRP) concepts. Offer both foundational training and advanced courses for those managing complex inventory processes.

2. Building Proficiency in Technology and Data Analysis

Technology plays a vital role in demand-driven inventory management, from AI-driven forecasting to IoT-based tracking. Ensuring that employees can navigate and fully leverage these tools maximizes the benefits of a data-driven approach.

Actionable Step: Implement regular training on inventory management software, forecasting tools, and data visualization. For example, offer hands-on workshops in which team members learn to interpret data trends, set reorder points, and monitor inventory KPIs using the company's chosen systems.

3. Creating an Agile and Adaptive Team Mindset

Demand-driven inventory management requires teams to be agile and ready to adjust to market shifts quickly. Training programs should emphasize adaptability and decision-making skills that allow employees to respond efficiently to sudden changes in demand or supply chain disruptions.

Actionable Step: Use scenario planning exercises and role-playing simulations to train staff on reacting to unexpected supply or demand changes. These exercises can help inventory teams develop a proactive, solution-oriented mindset that minimizes disruptions.

Setting Up for Long-Term Success in Demand-Driven Inventory Management

To ensure that demand-driven inventory management becomes a sustainable, value-adding component of the organization, it's critical to establish a foundation for continuous improvement, feedback loops, and alignment with long-term business goals. Here are several strategies for embedding demand-driven practices into the organizational fabric and setting the stage for ongoing success.

1. Establishing Continuous Improvement and Feedback Mechanisms

Demand-driven inventory management is an ongoing journey that requires refinement over time. By fostering a culture of continuous improvement, companies can regularly assess their strategies, processes, and technologies to stay aligned with evolving market demands.

Actionable Step: Implement regular review sessions where inventory teams analyze performance metrics, gather feedback, and discuss potential improvements. Encouraging teams to experiment with small-scale changes, such as testing new buffer strategies, can help identify improvements without causing disruption.

2. Aligning Inventory Management with Strategic Goals

Demand-driven inventory management should be integrated into the company's broader strategic objectives. Whether the organization prioritizes customer satisfaction, cost efficiency, or sustainability, aligning inventory strategies with these goals helps maximize their impact.

Actionable Step: Ensure inventory management goals are regularly reviewed in the context of overall business objectives. Incorporate these goals into strategic planning sessions and ensure that inventory teams understand how their work contributes to the company's success.

3. Leveraging Technology for Scalability and Future Growth

As demand-driven inventory management continues to evolve, companies need to remain open to new technologies and innovations that can enhance scalability and streamline processes. Technologies like AI, IoT, and advanced analytics can significantly bolster a company's ability to manage inventory more effectively.

Actionable Step: Set up a dedicated team to monitor and assess emerging technologies and recommend upgrades or integrations. Additionally, develop a technology roadmap for inventory management that outlines potential future investments in alignment with the company's growth strategy.

4. Celebrating Successes and Learning from Setbacks

Celebrating achievements and learning from challenges helps reinforce demand-driven principles within the organization. Acknowledging successful initiatives, like improved forecasting accuracy or reduced stockouts, can motivate employees and demonstrate the tangible benefits of a demand-driven approach.

Actionable Step: Implement a recognition program that celebrates teams or individuals who make significant contributions to inventory management improvements. Similarly, conduct "lessons learned" sessions to review setbacks, enabling teams to refine their approaches and avoid future issues.

Conclusion: Building a Demand-Driven Inventory Culture

Building a demand-driven inventory culture is a transformative endeavor that requires a strategic, cohesive approach from leadership and across all operational levels. Integrating demand-driven principles into the organizational culture, developing a skilled and adaptable workforce, and focusing on continuous improvement are essential steps toward creating a sustainable, competitive advantage in inventory management.

As companies implement and refine these practices, they set themselves up to not only respond effectively to current market demands but also to anticipate future changes with agility and confidence. In a world where supply chain disruptions, demand volatility, and customer expectations are constant challenges, a demand-driven culture equips companies to turn these challenges into opportunities for growth and differentiation. The organizations that successfully embrace and nurture this culture will be well-positioned to thrive in an increasingly complex and competitive market.